Congratulations for taking the first steps to finding out the Key ingredients that separate the Millionaires from the Strugglers! By doing so I would like to award you a certificate to attend my "Business Mastery—Power in YOU!" Program

Valued at $2,996

To register and for more information go to

www.MYMSuccess.com
or call (+1) 778-565-4090.

Use Success Number: _12922_
when you register.

(If there is not a Success Number above, quote CPID48)

ENTREPRENEUR SUCCESS RECIPE

Praise for
ENTREPRENEUR SUCCESS RECIPE

"Colin Sprake has delivered the goods. He not only provides the recipe for entrepreneurial success, he also lays out a clear-cut plan for how to get it. What I like best is that it's not just a bunch of theory. This book is jam-packed full of specific ideas for separating yourself from the pack. This book teaches you the necessary skills, instructions, and troubleshooting tactics unlike any other book out there. Do yourself a favor and get a copy of this book; then do what he says in it and take action."

JJ Childers, attorney and author of
Real Wealth without Risk and *Asset Protection 101*

"Colin Sprake has filled a book with solid and exceptionally readable advice. Implement his simple-to-follow suggestions, and life will be a whole lot more fun for you, especially when you make bank deposits."

Jay Conrad Levinson, bestselling author
and father of *Guerrilla Marketing*

"Finally, Colin has taken his decades of brilliance on combining mindset with business and put them together in an incredibly smart way, to assist all entrepreneurs with achieving outrageous levels of success. Plus, it's done in very simple and easy-to-follow format. You have got to read this book!"

Jill Lublin, international speaker and bestselling author of three books, including *Guerrilla Publicity*

"I could not put this book down! I have read countless books on entrepreneurship, yet what Colin has done with his direct style is engage you into knowing that you can achieve more and hit new heights in all areas of your life. Master these principles and be amazed by what you can achieve!"

David Hancock, Founder, Morgan James Publishing

"Finally, a perfect recipe for becoming a successful entrepreneur – make sure you follow it. This should have been done years ago! Colin is a genius at what he has put together to get all entrepreneurs to the next level of success. If you are an entrepreneur you have to read this book!"

Rick Frishman, bestselling author,
publisher, and speaker.

ENTREPRENEUR SUCCESS RECIPE

KEY INGREDIENTS THAT SEPARATE THE MILLIONAIRES FROM THE STRUGGLERS!

COLIN SPRAKE

NEW YORK

ENTREPRENEUR SUCCESS RECIPE
KEY INGREDIENTS THAT SEPARATE THE MILLIONAIRES FROM THE STRUGGLERS!

ISBN 978-1-61448-336-6 paperback
ISBN 978-1-61448-439-4 hard cover
ISBN 978-1-61448-337-3 eBook
Library of Congress Control Number: 2012948150

Morgan James Publishing
The Entrepreneurial Publisher
5 Penn Plaza, 23rd Floor,
New York City, New York 10001
(212) 655-5470 office • (516) 908-4496 fax
www.MorganJamesPublishing.com

Cover Design by:
Rachel Lopez
www.r2cdesign.com

In an effort to support local communities, raise awareness and funds, Morgan James Publishing donates a percentage of all book sales for the life of each book to Habitat for Humanity Peninsula and Greater Williamsburg.

Get involved today, visit
www.MorganJamesBuilds.com.

Habitat for Humanity®
Peninsula and
Greater Williamsburg
Building Partner

To my gorgeous wife Gabi,
my two gems Ruby and Jade,
and all the family, friends, mentors,
and students who have added to my
growth over the past thirty years

CONTENTS

INTRODUCTION

KNOWLEDGE + ACTION = PROFIT

SUCCESS
SPOTLIGHT!
Action is the bridge between
knowledge and profit!

Most of my friends know me as a serial entrepreneur. I've been running my own businesses since the young age of nine, and I know that there are so many things to consider when deciding to venture out on your own to start a business and take the entrepreneurial life by the horns. It's one of the biggest decisions you will make in your life, and if done right, it is extremely rewarding and fulfilling. But because there are so many unknowns before you even start out, this by itself can take many people out of the entrepreneurship game unnecessarily.

Being an entrepreneur takes many talents and skills; my goal is to take you on the same three-decade journey that I've been on to help you understand what true entrepreneurship is all about. I have learned a ton and figured out what it takes to be a truly SUCCESSFUL entrepreneur. My life experiences and what I call my "university fees of life" have in some instances cost me hundreds of thousands of dollars. If you have the skills, and understand what skills you need to learn and develop in order to be a successful entrepreneur, then you are on your path to massive success.

Since the age of nine, I have ventured out into many types of businesses: from cabinet making, handyman services, mining equipment, natural skin care, and pole dancing (for fitness), to my current business, Make Your Mark Training and Consulting, Inc., which trains and transforms businesses to achieve massive levels of success. Over the past several decades, I have worked with thousands of entrepreneurs, and I have discovered what separates those who become millionaires and live the dream lifestyle, and those who go broke, doing everything they can to make it. Yet those in the second group are only missing a few key ingredients that will dramatically improve their chances of living the lifestyle and earning the income they dream about. They only need to understand what they are.

In this book, you will learn what it takes to be an entrepreneur with the Entrepreneurial Success Recipe. Following a recipe is the best metaphor I know to describe what it takes to really succeed as an entrepreneur. For instance, if you want to bake a cake, you need to first make sure you have the right recipe: you need to make sure you're making something you want to eat! Second, you need to prepare your work area so you have all the space and equipment you need to follow the recipe. Third, you need to look at the ingredient list to see which ones you have and which ones you need. But even when you have everything the recipe calls for, that isn't enough. If you want the mouthwatering cake the recipe promises, you have to take action and DO something, don't you?

Similarly, in this book, first we'll make sure you know what an entrepreneur is—and whether you really want what this recipe will deliver! Second, you'll learn how to prepare for your entrepreneurial success by developing a success mindset. Third, you'll learn about the nineteen crucial ingredients (i.e., skills and habits) for entrepreneurial success and assess which ones you have and which ones you need with the Entrepreneurial Test. But again, it's not enough to know everything there is to know about starting and growing a business. You have to DO it. So then I'll show you exactly what to do to put these skills and habits into practice with a straightforward list of the fifteen things you must do after you read this book. Plus, you'll get a bonus most recipes don't give you. I've also included a troubleshooting section that explains the nine areas where most entrepreneurs' success tends to stall—when you think you've been following the recipe exactly, but something's still not working. It does take work, but it's fun, and I am pleased to assist you on your journey.

Like most recipes, it often takes a few attempts to get the perfect product, even if you do follow the instructions perfectly. You may look at the success recipe in this book and decide to alter it even before you have attempted it the first time. My advice to you is to follow the instructions a few times before you decide to alter or enhance the recipe. The ingredients and instructions have been created from decades of work and life experiences and are served to you on a golden platter to achieve the success you want without having to go through all the learning and costly mistakes.

Many people struggling in their own businesses, whether it is a traditional business, multilevel marketing business, or a franchise, do not even know that they are lacking in certain skills to become a successful entrepreneur. Sadly, in some instances they are too proud and often too stubborn to acknowledge that they do not have all the skills they need, and they would rather die defending their actions than learn from other successful business owners and entrepreneurs.

In fact, many entrepreneurs are technicians who worked for somebody else and now have gone out and started their own business in exactly the same field. A good example of this is a plumber who works for a company and then decides to go out and start his own plumbing business. He may be a good plumber, but who says he is a good entrepreneur or businessperson? Does he truly have what it takes? This goes for doctors, dentists, chiropractors, electricians, hairdressers, etc. They are all specialized in their fields, but often they have not received the training or tools to truly understand what it takes to be successful as a businessperson.

You may have heard the statistic that 80 percent of start-up businesses fail in the first year, and of the remaining 20 percent, 80 percent of them fail in their second year. This means that 96 percent of businesses fail in their first two years. Achieving your fifth anniversary is even more daunting, as only 1 percent of start-up businesses get to their fifth anniversary in a highly profitable state. Yes, you can say you are still alive at the five-year mark, but are you surviving or thriving?

The difference between surviving and thriving is taking the knowledge that you get from this book and start putting it into action immediately. You do not have to finish the book before you start taking action. In fact, you may read a chapter a week and implement the items as you go. Just get it done! In my training company, Make Your Mark, we live by the KAP principle: Knowledge, Action, and Profit. The principle is very simple: you will not profit from any knowledge you receive unless you take action as a result.

Action truly is the bridge between *knowledge* and *profit*.

Have fun, enjoy the journey, and become part of the 1 percent of truly successful entrepreneurs who celebrate their fifth anniversary in an extremely profitable position.

You are your success,

COLIN SPRAKE

Founder and Lead Trainer

Make Your Mark Training and Consulting, Inc.

PART ONE

PREPARATION

CHAPTER 1

WHAT IS AN
ENTREPRENEUR?

SUCCESS
SPOTLIGHT!
What you focus on
dictates your results.

W hen you're following a recipe, it's good to know what the recipe is for—and if it's what you really want to make! So, what are we going to end up with if we follow the Entrepreneurial Success Recipe? What is an entrepreneur? According to Wikipedia, an entrepreneur is an owner or manager of a business enterprise who makes money through risk and initiative. It is also a term applied to a person who is willing to help launch a new venture or enterprise and

3

accept full responsibility for the outcome. The key words in this definition are *risk, initiative,* and *responsibility.*

In fact, I sometimes sit back and chuckle at the challenges that we have as entrepreneurs. In order to be an entrepreneur, you have to be creative, which is a huge asset. Yet the only way you truly win is when you become laser focused on the goals you want to achieve.

Laser focus can only happen when you have a clear goal or target. Without a goal, you have nothing to aim at—being laser focused requires becoming dedicated (no matter what) to achieving a goal and not being taken out by distractions along the way. This is often one of the more challenging items for entrepreneurs. In fact, the statement "laser-focused entrepreneur" often is an oxymoron. How do you become a laser-focused entrepreneur? It all starts with your *mindset.*

CHAPTER 2

THE ENTREPRENEURIAL
MINDSET

SUCCESS
SPOTLIGHT!
Feel it to reveal it.

SELF-AWARENESS AND
SELF-OBSERVATION

As you begin your journey as an entrepreneur, the most important first step is to develop the right mindset. When I talk about your mindset, I'm talking about the way that you think, because the way that you think will dictate the results that you get in your business. I believe that your thoughts completely control your destiny in every aspect of your life. Thoughts are energy, whether conscious or subconscious, and what you put "out there" will show up in your life. This is known as the law of attraction.[1] Our life experiences as children and the habits we inherited from our parents or siblings dramatically impact who we are as adults and how we approach things, even as an entrepreneur.

Your thoughts completely dictate what is showing up in your life right now!

I hear thousands of different life-impacting statements that hinder people from achieving the success they deserve, and the sad part is most people do not even realize it.

Here are a few key examples:

- I am not good at that.
- It's tough in our industry right now!
- I cannot remember names.
- I hate looking at my numbers.
- People never return my phone calls.
- I am not good at doing videos.
- It's hard to find profitable clients.
- Our business is seasonal and we are slow in…
- The economy has changed.
- I don't like sales or selling.
- I keep on getting tough clients!

---

1   See Rhonda Byrne's *The Secret* (Simon & Schuster, 2006) and her movie by the same name. The "secret" this book describes is what many other books have referred to as the law of attraction, which says that whatever you believe, you tend to attract.

- I don't have the success formula.
- What you teach does not work in my industry.
- Mondays are put-out-fire days!

It's very simple. Until you start reframing these statements, you will continue to attract them into your life and business and will keep achieving the same results. Because your mind does not know right from wrong, it will just give you what you say and think about most.

So the first step to developing an entrepreneurial mindset is to simply become more self-aware. What kinds of things do you find yourself saying or thinking? Do they support your success in your business and your life, or do they sabotage it?

You can use this self-awareness in every aspect of your life and business. The more self-aware and self-observant you become about what you are saying and thinking, the more you will increase the success in your own life. You have to realize that nine out of ten thoughts are negative in the society we live in, and keeping your thoughts positive takes a ton of self-awareness and corrective action. Many of us often do not even realize how negative our own words are. Sadly, what we are saying is what is showing up in our lives and businesses.

STINKING THINKING

SUCCESS
SPOTLIGHT!
You cannot determine your standings in a race until you cross the finish line.

Once you become more aware of your automatic thoughts and understand how they impact your business, you may find that you're like 95 percent of other struggling entrepreneurs I encounter: you have "stinking thinking." If most of your thoughts are sabotaging your business, the most important change you can make is to look at all your experiences and all the choices you've made in a positive light. Let's look at the three words below:

- Right
- Success
- Good

What are the opposites, or antonyms, of these three words? Yes: wrong, failure, and bad! I can guarantee you one thing as you go out and start building your business: there will be challenges along the way. It's how you look at these challenges and the choices that you make, and what you learn from them, that will dictate the results and success in every given situation! I strongly believe that challenges are put to us to see if we can handle them and to make us stronger for future challenges! Most entrepreneurs often give up or throw in the towel when the challenges get too tough, and often you do not even realize that you may be one powerful decision away from achieving incredible success and greatness. Yet you stop because of fear and pain! You must understand that you cannot determine your standing in a race until you cross the finish line. If you do not cross the finish line, you have not given yourself the opportunity to determine your results and learn what needs to be done to improve.

So instead of using the words *wrong, failure,* and *bad,* replace them with the word LEARNING! You're not going to know everything when you first start out in business, and it's good to understand that you should not chastise yourself for every learning experience that you have. The most important part is to make sure that they *are* learning experiences, and that you figure out what you have learned from them in order not to make the same mistake twice.

Even the words you use can impact you emotionally and have you feeling differently about certain experiences. In one of my businesses, I had a line of credit for close to $300,000. Because of various market situations and incredible challenges within the business, we had to shut the business down, and I was left with the debt. I decided to rename the debt account the Power Education Fund to shift the energy around it and how I thought about it! I learned a ton from the $300,000 debt, and I can tell you that I would not be where I am today if I had not taken the learning experiences from the situation. In fact, it has allowed me to build a very strong and lucrative Pro CEO Consulting practice, as I now fully understand what my clients are going through and what can be done to assist them.

The way you frame things and the words you use will dramatically impact your long-term success.

Here's another example. If you say you cannot remember names, guess what: you will never be able to remember names, because you keep on reinforcing your mind's belief that you cannot remember names every time you say it. The more you say self-defeating statements, the more you ingrain them into your being. Just like computers, our thought processes are our programming. The more you program your mind, body, and cells with powerful life-enhancing statements, the more they will be delivered to you, and your success will skyrocket. On the contrary, some people do not even realize they are constantly putting viruses into their programming, and it's directly proportional to the results that they are achieving.

On the other hand, when you catch yourself saying or thinking statements that are self-defeating or not supportive of your life or your business, you cannot just go from one extreme to the other. If you simply start saying, "I am great at remembering names," your mind will subconsciously say "bullshitter," and you will revert back to your common belief.

What you need to say is, "I am in the process of remembering all names." Your subconscious mind can accept this, as it is plausible, and the more you say it, the more you will believe it, and the better you will become at remembering names.

If you are continually thinking about your debt or lack of results, guess what: they will continue to show up! You have to really start to reprogram yourself and get into new, supportive success statements in all areas of your life. And I mean all areas of your life! Even when you say things about yourself in jest, you are truly programming your mind and body. Simple statements like "Sometimes I am so stupid," or "I was such an idiot today!" are all non-supportive statements that, if said enough, will manifest into your reality on a regular basis. You have to be truly aware of absolutely everything you say and think!

Be careful, though, as you do not want to focus on what you don't want. If you keep on having difficult clients, rather than saying, "I am finding fewer difficult clients," say, "I have amazing money-making, highly profitable clients coming my way." If you say, "I am finding fewer difficult clients," your brain is still focused on the difficult clients, and they will continue to show up. In the movie version of *The Secret,* this is clearly explained by the late Mother Teresa, who always said she would go to a peace rally but never an anti-war rally—if you focus on anti-war, you get war! What you resist persists!

TAKING THINGS
PERSONALLY

SUCCESS
SPOTLIGHT!
A client who voices an opinion
is an asset.

This is the most important skill that I had to learn in my own business. For example, recently a few clients wrote to me to say that they had some challenges with the groups they belonged to that were part of our company. Now, I could have gotten very upset. It was at the start of the year, and my mind automatically thought, *WOW! What a way to start the New Year!* But when I started to take things personally, I took a step back and said to myself, "What am I meant to learn from these amazing clients voicing their opinions to me?"

You could simply say that they were disgruntled clients, but to me, these are some of the most important assets that you have in your business when you are first starting out. A client who voices his opinion is an asset, because so many clients never voice their opinions directly to you, but instead do it in front of other people, and this harms your reputation and that of your business. If they voice their opinions directly to you, you can take the corrective action to improve your business, improve your systems, and overall make your client experience excellent.

The learning experiences I took from these situations have allowed me to examine how our business education groups are operating and to ensure that our students are receiving extreme value for their money and time. You have to realize that your client's perception of you and your business is reality. No matter what you think they are thinking about you and your business, until you ask them, you will never know. I hold an annual Master Mind event at a high-end exclusive venue, where we invite twenty-five select clients to come out and share a day with us as we present Make Your Mark and our plans for the next twelve months, and we ask them for feedback and input. They are not there to direct our business, just to give us feedback on what we are thinking about improving and enhancing. It's the most vulnerable that I ever am in front of our clients. Yet the input we receive is an integral part of our continued success as a company. I would highly recommend that every business do this on an annual basis and listen to what its clients have to say. You do not have to implement everything that they recommend or suggest. This kind of feedback simply gives you a barometer to measure where you are as a company.

You see, it is the way that you think and the thoughts that you have that will either grow your business substantially, cause it to struggle, or at worst, run it into the ground. The above concept is very simple and sounds very easy to implement, but it requires diligence to successfully apply it to your business. So my challenge to you is to catch yourself in the process of negative thoughts and ask yourself, "What am I meant to learn from this experience, situation, or choice that I made, in order to make my business stronger and dramatically improve my relationships with my customers?"

Your customers can teach you a lot, and one of the most important things to understand is that you need to take your own ego out of the equation; put it aside and listen to your prospects and clients. By listening to them, you will grow your business faster and stronger and more sustainably.

TEFLON, NOT VELCRO

SUCCESS
SPOTLIGHT!
Success is the result of specific events and, more importantly, how you perceive those events.

Taking things personally is one thing, but how long you hold on to these things is 100 percent your choice! You've heard many people say, "I am having a bad day." My question is, does it have to be a bad day, or can it just be a bad moment, a bad few minutes, or a bad hour? It is 100 percent your choice how long you hold on to these given situations and how you respond to everything that is said or done to you. In fact, taking the advice from earlier in the chapter, you should be looking at it not as "bad," but in terms of what you can *learn* from these given situations.

Remember, success is caused both by specific events and by how you perceive events. Your perception of how things look is sometimes completely slanted.

A good example is when you go to visit a client and anticipate taking their order or signing the contract, and things do not go the way you thought they would. The client ends up trying to beat you down on price, or not giving you the terms that you want, or possibly just not signing the contract, and you walk away with no order. Many people take these situations extremely personally, when they should be asking, "What can I learn from the situation, and what was my contribution to the given situation?" Consider simple things like the following:

- How can I prepare more effectively the next time?
- What research could I have done to improve the situation?
- What needs to be done to ensure it does not happen again?

If you have done all of the above and you still do not get the contract, do not beat yourself up, but rather say,

"NEXT," and move on to somebody who has a greater potential of becoming your customer.

What I really want you to get from this is that how you approach every situation will determine the outcome and results you achieve. You can either look at everything as a learning experience, or let your ego kick in and arrogance take over and not care about what anybody has to say! From my experience, this will be the demise of your business, because without clients you have nothing. Your clients pay your bills and give you the lifestyle that you have and want. Always be sure to show gratitude towards your clients on a regular basis!

Simply decide every time somebody comments about you and your business whether you are wearing a Teflon suit or a Velcro suit. When comments are thrown at you, are you going to wear a Teflon suit and let them just slide off, or are you going to wear a Velcro suit and let them stick to you? This is not, however, a time to be arrogant—some comments you receive are extremely valuable to your business and you should see them in that light. It's just how they personally affect you that you have to be careful of.

Wearing a Velcro suit can hinder you from achieving the most incredible success, because you let things take you down. Instead, wear a Teflon suit, and realize that in many situations, you are the one who has decided to take things personally and allow them to bring you down.

BE A RHINO

SUCCESS SPOTLIGHT!

You have to be able to handle comments from people, even those close to you, and stay true to your plan.

Not only should you frequently wear a Teflon suit, but you should also ensure it is a thick suit that does not allow things to penetrate it. You have to have a thick skin, like a rhino.

As you grow your business, you have to let things bounce off you. As entrepreneurs, one of the key areas that sometimes hinders us is that our family focuses too much on how many hours we're trading for dollars, or they believe we should be doing something else with our lives. The life of an entrepreneur is all about trading many hours in the beginning for few dollars, and as you grow and become extremely successful, you trade few hours for many dollars. I suppose you could call this the entrepreneurial dream! The only way you achieve this, though, is by having a plan!

There will always be people in your life whose words will impact you deeply, and you have to decide if you want to listen to them. Some people may tell you that if you are not successful after a few months, you should just get a job; or they may tell you that your business idea is flawed, etc. You have to be able to handle comments from people, even those close to you, and stay true to your plan.

CELEBRATE AS IF IT
HAS ALREADY HAPPENED

SUCCESS
SPOTLIGHT!
When you focus on money you will have dollars to count. When you focus on people you will have countless dollars.

This is one of the more advanced levels of mind training: celebrate as if the success has already happened. Doing so opens up your life and allows things to enter your experience. When you are in your office and writing a proposal, you should be celebrating in your mind as if you have already won the proposal—and not be anxiously wondering what will happen when you send the proposal through. You need to send it off with positive energy and good intentions, as if you have already won the project, bid, etc. When you start to feel it in your body and really program your thinking to believe that you have already won, you will start to win more orders, projects, contracts, etc. than you ever have.

The most important part of this concept is to focus on what winning is going to do for *your client*. Do not let your ego get in the way and become totally focused on the money. The universe has a very powerful way of keeping things in equilibrium, and if you only focus on winning purely for the money, you may win the contract, but as quickly as the money comes in, a tax bill or something else comes in to keep things in balance.

I live by the statement: "When you focus on money, you will have dollars to count; when you focus on people, you will have countless dollars."

Every time I win a big Pro CEO Consulting contract or a speaking engagement and I receive the deposit check, I do get very excited, but at the same time, I hold the check in my hands and look at it and visualize what I am going to be able to do for the client because of the check. It really feels great when you start to feel the results before you have actually delivered what has been proposed. Remember, you are the expert in your area, and you know you are going to deliver amazing products and/or services that are going to assist people in their lives or businesses, so it should be very easy for you to visualize the results you are going to deliver—even seeing the satisfied look on your clients' faces and celebrating what you have delivered.

I even do it with every e-mail that I send out. I send each and every e-mail out with love and light and ask the universe to have the e-mail impact the people it is meant to, as I know what our trainings will do for people in their lives and businesses. I send great intentions with the e-mail, and I do this especially with all our database marketing e-mails that go out.

In some instances, you may do all of the above and still not win the project, and then start to believe that these principles do not work. They most definitely work—it is just a matter of you believing that they do. Also, sometimes you lose a big project, order, contract, etc. because you were maybe not ready for it, or possibly you were meant to learn something from the experience.

Like I said earlier, you need to ask yourself why things have happened and what you were meant to learn from the experience. When you start to do this with everything— and I mean *everything*—in your life, you will start to really understand how to move things forward at an accelerated rate, because you will not allow things to affect you and take you out of the game!

Business is just like rugby or any sport; you cannot improve your game without practicing and being involved in the game fully—both physically and mentally. All great sports stars will tell you that mindset is the biggest asset you have, and it is probably 95 percent of the reason why they win or lose. You can have the best skills in the world, but if your mind is not in the game, you will not perform your best, and you will easily be taken out by some of the simplest negative thoughts. It is no different in business! You can read this entire book, and at the end you will realize that you are the only person in control of your destiny—you cannot blame it on someone else, lack of money, or anything! You can only blame yourself if you do not succeed.

As you read this, you may be saying that lack of money is hindering your progress. This may be so, but until you start to realize that you are surrounded by abundance and that you can always find money from someone, you will only keep reinforcing your belief that your lack of success is because of money, rather than putting a plan together and going out to find an investor to assist you in your business. You may have other mindset hurdles that come after you eliminate the money hurdle, such as how do I put a plan together, or where would I find these investors? These are all hurdles that we will talk about in a later chapter.

In the past few years, one of the major ice hockey teams hired a success celebration coach, and all they did was skate past the bench where the other players were sitting and high-five each other and celebrate as if they had just scored a goal. They would do this at every practice session and continued to do this until the feeling of scoring and celebrating was ingrained in them. It opened up their minds to want to celebrate, and it also opens up the universe to give you a reason to celebrate. This may sound outrageous or ridiculous, but when you open up to receiving in your life, things will show up as long as you believe it.

And you must feel it to reveal it!

When you truly start to believe that something is going to happen, and you get out of your head and into your heart, you will start to internalize the belief and really feel the feelings of what is coming. Your body does not care whether they are negative or positive feelings. Whatever you give your attention to and start to feel in your throat, neck, torso, or gut will show up. Many people do not believe in the law of attraction, but they fail to see that what they feel on a daily basis becomes the results they receive and achieve on a daily basis. When you truly get out of your head and into the feelings of success, sometimes long before it comes, the results that are revealed directly relate to your feelings. The law of attraction shows up in ALL our lives every day, whether we believe it or not.

That ice hockey team went on to win the coveted Stanley Cup trophy that year. It really is all about feeling the success!

At our three-day Business Mastery—Power in YOU! event, we go through a very specific experiential exercise that gets participants out of their heads and into the feelings around success. And it amazes me what people say when they really feel their success! Pete, a student, said the following after going through this exercise: "I cannot believe how I feel. Every part of my body is tingling with excitement. I feel like it has happened and as if my whole being is in alignment with the results I want to achieve. It's awesome!"

Yes, our heads are the thought center for our feelings, and our feelings dictate our results—they are all intertwined!

In fact, I call our head the "editor" for our hearts and guts. Most people do not realize it, but we have around 100 billion neurons in our brains. When a stomach was dissected in a recent experiment, the scientists determined that the stomach wall has around 100 million neurons in it, which includes twenty-one of the same neuron types as the brain. This means that your stomach is a thought center. Why do you think we say "listen to your gut"? Your gut may actually be a stronger thought center than your brain, because it does not have that powerful editor called the mind to alter the decisions or filter them. It is common to hear someone say, "I had a gut feeling about that situation," or "I should have followed my gut." Now you know why. Similarly, scientists are also discovering that the heart tissue is very similar to that of the brain and also has some of the same neurons as the brain. We really should trust our hearts and guts more!

ENTREPRENEURS
ARE ADDICTS

SUCCESS
SPOTLIGHT!
Be aware of what addictions are stopping your greatness.

I believe that we are all creatures of habit and that our lives are simply a series of habits. Some habits support success, and others impede it! In order to move your business to the next level and change the results you are achieving, you have to significantly change your non-supportive or negative habits.

I call these negative habits "addictions," because you may be holding on to these habits of thought or behavior and feel they are aiding you, but from the outside others can see that they are habits that will never build success. This is very much like being an alcoholic, and until you decide to check into rehab, you are not going to eliminate the poor, non-supportive habits. A lot of our courses have the name "warrior" in them, and I joke with many of our students that I'm planning to add Intervention Warrior Courses, so business owners and entrepreneurs can check into business rehab and really eliminate the non-supportive habits from their lives and businesses.

Do you have addictions and habits that are non-supportive and are holding you back from achieving greatness in your business and life?

The biggest part of overcoming addictions is to first admit that you have a problem, and from there take the necessary action in order to overcome the challenges. Sadly, most business owners and entrepreneurs never acknowledge that they are addicted to certain non-supportive behaviors and habits that keep them in the same place, achieving the same results.

Below are some key addictions that I have experienced in my decades of working with entrepreneurs and some that I have had to overcome myself:

- Being too stubborn to take advice.
- Taking advice from successful people and then deciding not to use it.
- Making excuses and finding reasons why things are not getting done.
- Blaming others for lack of success or for inherent behaviors.
- Continually justifying why things work a certain way in their industry and not being open to ideas that may dramatically improve their business.
- Focusing on getting and not giving.
- Repeatedly saying self-destructive words and phrases.
- Being quick to defend, justify, and explain every situation or event!

It's good to be aware of what addictions are stopping you from achieving your greatness and finding the right places and programs in order to overcome them and get yourself to the next level.

It will take work to overcome some of these challenges. What you need to decide on today is: Where do you want to be twelve months from now, and what you are going to do to get there? What new supportive habits and addictions are you going to create that build you up and create more success in your life? It's all part of adding the right ingredients to achieving the success you want!

RESPONSIBILITY

SUCCESS
SPOTLIGHT!
When we point one finger forward, three fingers are pointing back at us.

It all starts in childhood: from a very young age, we learn to point fingers at other people who have not been good to us or who have done something against us, and the blame game begins. But what we do not realize is that when we point one finger forward, three fingers are pointing back at us. The sad part for us as children is that we learn a lot of our habits and inborn traits (whether we like them or not) from our parents.

And our parents are only a product of a developed society. The reason why I say a "developed" society is because in the underdeveloped world, people have very specific tasks that they have to do every single day, and for most of them, they're survival related, like looking for food and water. They take responsibility for what needs to be done in their own lives. In developed nations, we have governments that are deeply in debt, and because of these leadership decisions and mismanagement of funds, the majority of these developed nations have terrible debt situations with their people. I often say, if we were to run our businesses the same way as most governments, we would have an even higher rate of business failure!

People are living in a state of fear, wondering how they are going to retire and have enough money to do so. Many people believe that they will win the lottery, or perhaps they can even sue somebody to have enough funds to live the dream lifestyle. We live in a very litigious society, where some people believe that they should take advantage of other people by suing them whenever possible, rather than taking responsibility for their involvement in the given situation.

A recent example was when a lady wanted to sue the municipality because she tripped on a curb that was not built to exactly the right height, and she broke her leg. I feel this is getting ridiculous and wonder when it is going to stop. People really need to start taking responsibility for their actions. If you slip on a curb and break your leg, you should be asking yourself, "What did I learn from this experience, and how can I avoid this situation next time?" No, instead many people look for all avenues to blame other people, whether that's individuals, municipalities, governments, companies, absolutely anybody... other than ourselves! I fully agree that legal action is appropriate in some situations. The sad part about it is that there are many lawyers around, looking for situations where they can play the blame game and line their pockets. In fact, society as a whole is deeply embedded in the "one finger forward, three fingers back" blame game. We spend most of our day blaming other people for things that they did not do, or things that they did do, or for the lack of results! This is the one finger pointing forward! Heaven forbid that we should blame ourselves for a given situation or our results. (In reality, these are the three fingers pointing back.)

The truth is that we play a part in every situation that arises in our lives through our own choices. And when we start to shift toward taking responsibility, we will start to see amazing results. It all starts with each individual taking responsibility for his own actions in every life situation.

Once you're on this glorious planet called Earth, everything that comes your way is 100 percent because of the choices that you make. It doesn't matter whether it's at home, in school, in business, or anywhere else in life. The reason why you are where you are today is purely because of the choices that you have made. Many people believe that the situations they are in are all somebody else's responsibility. As you go through the examples later in the book, you'll start to realize that you had choices in all the situations you have been in, and it was your choice to be part of them.

It is extremely enlightening to realize that you have thoughts every single day, and because of these thoughts you make choices, and those choices will dictate your future results.

Many people seem to think that the choices that they have made are somebody else's responsibility. They live their lives blaming other people for their situations. And the moment they start to realize that their situations are 100 percent a result of their actions and choices, the quicker things will change for them and their lives. It's not about the blame game; it's all about us taking responsibility and realizing that we play a part of every single situation. We did not get there by chance, we got there by choice…our own choice!

One key to understanding the "one finger forward, three fingers back" is the concept of karma. Karma simply means that what you do to others comes back to you. When you do negative things to people and wonder why negative things are showing up in your life, it's karma. I heard a story recently of a gentleman who was busy robbing a convenience store, and the store owners were able to alert the police, who came around and arrested the gentleman in the act. While he was busy being arrested inside the convenience store, somebody else stole the thief's vehicle that was parked outside the convenience store. Now, that's karma!

The sooner we realize that we should take responsibility for all our actions and that we are intimately involved in all situations, the sooner this world will change for the better. I have written a twenty-five-page free e-book on this exact topic and how it impacts you both in your business and in life. You can download it at www.1forward3back.com. You will start to realize that the human mind is the only source of unhappiness on this planet!

During the summer, I host a party for our KAP-IT Success and BEST Mindset Groups. While I was setting up for this event, I had a huge self-awareness moment. A friend of mine had gifted me one hundred cans of beer for the event and had put them into the dollhouse on our property for me to access when I needed them. I went into the dollhouse to see what kind of beer they were, and I was upset that he had given me light beer. Not thinking about it again, and still being dissatisfied that they were light beer, I went back to the pool area to continue the setup for the event. About an hour later, I went running up to go and get the beer and put it in the coolers. I went running into the dollhouse, which has only a three-foot-high door, and ducked down to enter—but not enough. I cracked my head open and almost lost consciousness. Thank God I did not. I ran as quickly as I could, with blood gushing out of my head, to the rear door of my home and screamed for my wife. Both my daughters came running to meet me, and of course by this stage, I was completely drenched in blood.

I was rushed to the hospital by two very good friends, and they asked what had happened. I said, "Karma." They are both very in tune with their thoughts and attractions, just like me, and they said, "What do you mean?" I told them the story, and I said that the injury was for lack of gratitude!

When you become this self-aware and self-observant, your life will change, because you will really start to realize how powerful every thought is. Every event that happens in your life is directly proportional to the energy that you put out.

CHAPTER 3

COLIN SPRAKE'S STORY: FROM BLUE COLLAR TO
ENTREPRENEUR!

Everything you read in this book is what I have implemented in my own life and business, and it has taken me to the top of the entrepreneurial curve. I want the same for you and your business, and I know it can be done. So as we conclude this section on how to develop the right mindset for entrepreneurial success, consider my life story to be the picture on the recipe—proof that following the recipe really does produce the results you want!

I am South African by birth and moved to Canada in 1998. In my early, formative years, I lived in Johannesburg with my parents, brother, and sister. Both my mom and my dad believed that you had to go out and get highly educated, get a job, and work for that company for a long time. For many years I believed this, yet inside of me was a yearning to start my own business. I started to work for a hardware store at the age of nine and worked there until I was twenty-two years old. During this time I ran a paper route and was the fresh-produce manager for a large chain store. I got a lot of firsthand experience of what it was like to work for somebody else, and this was the start of my journey to find a way to educate myself in how to start my own business.

My mom and dad are still together after forty-seven years of marriage, and I have seen them go through some incredibly challenging times. We did not have a ton of money as I grew up. My dad did what he could with a grade ten education and was extremely successful as he went out and built a career in the medical equipment field.

My mom is an amazing lady who has struggled with depression for as long as I can remember. This depression resulted in her being negative in many of her thoughts, which surrounded us as we grew up, and still to this day I am amazed at how I turned out. Yet much of my work involves demonstrating to people that you can alter your thoughts no matter what environment you grew up in.

My dad traveled many days of the year and was seldom home, and I think something inside of me said, "I do not want to be this way when I grow up." This started me on my entrepreneurial path. I started a cabinetmaking company when I was eighteen years old, and my dad forced me to sell it when I was twenty years old in order to finish my studies in metallurgical engineering. I still thank him every day for doing this, as I would not be where I am today and may have been on a completely different path. This was meant to be, as I am living my passion and watching people transform every day, which is so exhilarating for me!

I completed my studies in metallurgical engineering in 1991 and did a business course which I finished in 1993. I moved to Vancouver, Canada, in 1998 with my gorgeous wife to join a metallurgical equipment manufacturer. I started traveling the world extensively, and by the age of thirty I had traveled to over seventy countries. During this time I took over the reins and became CEO, and I started to travel even more.

This started to wear thin, as my family would say to me, "You're just like your father." Plus, when my first daughter, Ruby, was four-and-a-half years old, she sat on my knee and said to me, "Daddy, when are you going to stop all the traveling?" At this stage, I had seen her for a total of about seven months in her short lifetime.

This interchange, combined with my entrepreneurial yearning to return to a business that was 100 percent my own, impacted me so dramatically that I decided to start a business that didn't require substantial travel and that allowed me to be home with my family 90 percent of the time. Since then, I've owned and operated businesses in the areas of fitness and cosmetics, and today I own and operate Make Your Mark, one of the fastest-growing business and personal-growth training companies in North America.

Yet my biggest challenge was still to come. In 2008, after my wife and I had invested hundreds of thousands of dollars into our own natural skin care line, the market crashed. We were heavily exposed in the United States, and within a matter of months we watched all our hard work and money vaporize, as retail stores discounted prices dramatically and we hit one of the worst recessions in North America. This drained a ton of our financial resources, and we hit rock bottom—for the first time in my life. I had to rely on all my mindset training and tools to get myself back on track, because the negative thoughts were rampant.

I looked at the close to $400,000 of skin-care products in our garage, and I knew that going back to retail would be a really tough sell in the current economic environment. I told my wife that I was going to create a gift basket company and create spa gift baskets, and Luxurious Corporate Gifts was launched. We did $150,000 in gift baskets in three months (October, November, and December). My wife continued to run this business for the same three months each year for the next three years, while I built Make Your Mark. Gabi now enjoys looking after our two amazing daughters and working part-time for Make Your Mark.

You will sometimes hear me say to people that they can take away my material goods and possessions, yet one thing that they cannot take away is my power mindset, the business knowledge that I have been gifted with, and my determination. In fact, one student asked me recently, if for some unforeseen reason Make Your Mark failed today, what would happen? My simple response was that now that I have mastered the tools in the Entrepreneur Success Recipe,

I would be back on my feet within a few weeks, earning tens of thousands of dollars a month.

The above experiences have shaped who I am today, and I hope that you can draw from your personal experiences and make decisions that are important to you and your family as you continue on the path of becoming an entrepreneur.

I've gone into substantial detail about who I am because I really want you to understand that being an entrepreneur is not easy, and many people fail at their first attempt. They often lose substantial money and even sometimes go bankrupt chasing their dream of a successful business.

This is truly the reason why I put my heart and all of my experiences into this book. I really want you to be able to put what you learn from this book into action, ensuring that you're not one of the casualties of entrepreneurship, but one of the amazing success stories, even as you approach your first business!

PART TWO

THE INGREDIENTS

CHAPTER 4

THE ENTREPRENEUR TEST: DO YOU HAVE
WHAT IT TAKES?

Entrepreneurship is not for everybody, and it's good to understand from the start the critical skills you need to become a truly successful entrepreneur. If you see a recipe for a dessert you'd like to try, and then notice that its main ingredient is coconut (and you hate coconut), you'll likely decide that this recipe isn't for you and keep looking for one that fits your tastes better. And even if you love coconut and decide to make it that very day, you still need to take stock of what ingredients you already have and what you need to get, so you do not get to the store and buy a lot of one ingredient you already had and none at all of the others!

So to make sure this is a recipe you want to follow, and to find out which ingredients for entrepreneurial success you already have (and which ones you'll need to get), I invite you to take the Entrepreneur Test below. Here is how it works:

Answer the following questions by putting a number in the right-hand column that indicates directly where you are today—not what you want in the future. The answer can be anywhere between 0 and 10. I would recommend taking the test in five minutes and writing down the scores that first come to mind. Do not overthink it. Be honest with yourself, as this will assist you with achieving the success you want and determining which ingredients you need to add or enhance.

Here is the scale:

0: No, or have not done this, or do not have the skill.
10: Yes, or absolutely have this done, or I have this skill and utilize it daily.

Again, answer the questions without thinking about them too much. Put down the number that first comes into your head, because that is often the most truthful number.

Critical Entrepreneurial Questions	Number
Do you have a business plan written down for the next twelve months?	
Do you have a vivid vision for your business that is written down?	
When bright, shiny objects distract you, do you stay focused on the task you've scheduled, rather than easily going off on a tangent?	
Do you LOVE going out and meeting people?	

Do you have set office hours and social time?	
As a leader, do you consistently motivate and inspire those working for you and with you, rather than complaining to them?	
Do you have a written sacrifice plan for your business?	
Do you use your time effectively and only have meetings that will grow your business?	
Do you have a clear written plan to achieve what you desire for your business, rather than merely wishing for it?	
When you learn things, do you implement immediately (10), or do you procrastinate (0)?	
Are you good at finding solutions for challenges, rather than allowing them to become hurdles?	
Who do you get advice from the most (spouse or non-entrepreneur = 0, highly successful mentors = 10)?	
Do you listen to advice, process it and implement accordingly?	
When you take a risk to invest in your business, do you focus on the rewards that will come from your investment, rather than the penalty?	
How passionate are you about what you do?	
Do you consistently take the same time to respond to clients, no matter how busy you are?	
Do you follow up with prospects and clients every time within 24 hours?	

Do you consistently portray energy, courtesy, and a winning attitude in every interaction you have?	
Do you spend more than 65 percent of your time in sales and marketing?	
TOTAL:	

Now that you have answered the questions, let's take a look at the results:

Your Score:	Path to Entrepreneurial Success
0-95	You need to decide if you have what it takes to be an entrepreneur. You have a ton to learn and implement, and you need to get going immediately!
96-133	You have some of the key items in place and need to really hone in on a few items in order to be a massively successful entrepreneur. You will know which ones they are from your answers.
134-190	You have the skill set to be a massively successful entrepreneur. You are well on your path to entrepreneurial success. Tweak a few skills, keep on learning, and grow professionally. There will be some key nuggets in the following chapter to assist you and give you more clarity and focus.

The subsequent chapter directly relates to each of the above questions and will assist you in adding or adjusting the ingredients you need to complete the Entrepreneur Success Recipe.

CHAPTER 5

NINETEEN CRITICAL SKILLS FOR ENTREPRENEURIAL
SUCCESS

Now that you've taken the test and have identified which entrepreneurial skills and habits you have (and which ones you need to develop), let's talk about them in more detail. If even one ingredient is missing, the recipe just won't turn out right, so it's good to understand why each one is critical to your success!

CREATE A ROAD MAP
TO SUCCESS

SUCCESS
SPOTLIGHT!
All goals are achievable; it's
just the time frame is often
unrealistic.

You have heard many times that if you fail to plan, then you plan to fail. This is a very true statement. Many people seldom plan the year ahead and wonder why, when they get to the end of the year, they have not achieved the results that they were wanting, whether it is in their personal life or in their business.

A study was conducted at Harvard School of Business where they took a group of MBA graduates and divided them into two separate groups; one group was to set goals and plans for the next five years, and the other group was to do no planning or goal setting. They went back five years later and interviewed the two separate groups, and found with no surprise that the group that did the planning and goal setting was earning nearly double that of their counterparts who had done no goal setting or planning.

This demonstrates how important it is to plan and set goals for the year ahead. You may not achieve all of them throughout the year, but at least you have something to aim for. You must understand that all goals are achievable; it's just that our time frame is often unrealistic. Having no written goals or plans is like going to an archery range with your crossbow in hand, loading in your arrow, and setting up to shoot at something—with no target in front of you! So, what do you aim for? There is no bull's-eye or any other part of the target for you to judge your results; you might as well just shoot the arrow in the air and hope that you hit something! This is not the way to operate your life or business.

The most important thing you can do is sit down and plan your year ahead. In fact, in my business we have a very specialized one-page business plan that we use to operate and manage our business for the year ahead. It is constructed from a number of different documents, and then summarized onto a single page so that you have a document that is easy to follow, simple to understand, and can guide you for the year ahead. You can even use the structure of the document to do your personal planning, too.

There are many theories out there about the perfect business plan. The way I look at things is that I would rather have a one-page business plan and a five-year vision for my business. Yes, if you're going to a bank for financing or looking for investors, then you need substantially more than a one-page business plan. But for managing your business, growing substantially, and monitoring your success, a one-page business plan is more than adequate for you to guide your success by. It becomes your reference tool by which you can measure your success for the year.

I have put all the tools for the one-page business plan on a website for you to download for free at www.My1PagePlan. com. It will take you about an hour or so to go through it in detail. All you need is to ensure is that you do it. It's fun to put a plan in place, because it truly is the difference between the successful millionaires and the strugglers.

DEVELOP VIVID VISION

SUCCESS SPOTLIGHT!

Creating a vivid vision is truly understanding what race you want to be in.

When you have a vivid vision for where you are going, you will always get somewhere and achieve incredible results. When you have a target, you know where to aim. When you have no target, you can aim anywhere and hope and pray to get a result. I have watched this happen, and I find it amazing that some people want success, yet they do not know how to get there or even have a simple road map for achieving success. Without a target, you're running your business by the seat of your pants! Getting up in the morning and deciding what to do for the day is operating your business from a to-do list, rather than from a written down, crystal-clear vision of where you want to be. I often ask students to write down their "to-be" list as part of developing a vivid vision.

Your vision for your business should be crystal clear, and you should know exactly what you want to achieve and why you are doing it. It's just like going out to win the hundred-meter dash. You have to have the right shoes, outfit, sleep, food, etc., to ensure you are in peak condition to give yourself the best chance of outrunning the competitors. It is no different in business; you must have all the tools, skills, processes, and systems in place to give yourself the best chance of achieving the win you want from your business.

Sadly, most business owners do not even know what race they are running. They wake up on the morning of the race, knowing they have a race and are unprepared, and arrive at the track wondering which race they have the best chance of winning according to the limited preparation they have done.

Creating a vivid vision is truly understanding what race you want to be in and creating and preparing everything that you need in order to give you the best chance of success, and it happens months, if not years, before the event.

If an athlete had to wake up on the day of a race with no major preparation done, how successful do you think he or she would be?

WEAPONS OF MASS DISTRACTION: AVOID BRIGHT, **SHINY OBJECTS**

SUCCESS SPOTLIGHT!

Take one business and give it laser focus, and watch how dramatically different your results will be.

Focus keeps you on track and ensures that you are always aiming in the direction of your vivid vision. The more focused you are, the less likely you are going to be impacted by distractions and the more successful your business will be. You also have to give your business, products, or services a chance to be successful. Do not give up easily. Be tenacious. You started with a passion, and if you do not make sales, you should not lose your passion. Keep that vivid vision of what you set out to do, and go and get it! There will always be challenges and learning experiences along the way—it's what you do with them that's important. By flipping from one product to another, or adding new items or services without having huge sales and success with what you have, you will always be struggling, because obviously you do not have a vivid vision for where you are going.

Just like the athlete, you have to practice on the same track for many years before you can proudly stand on the Olympic podium with the gold medal around your neck. This is the athlete's vision when he first starts out, and he stays true to that vision until it is achieved. What is your gold-medal vision for your business, and are you going to stay true to it until you achieve it? Most business owners I meet have no plan or vision for their business, and before they have even run the race a few times, they are looking at changing tracks or moving to another event before they have even given themselves the chance to win. Just like a recipe, you have to determine what delicious product you want, go and get the ingredients, and follow the instructions until you achieve the desired result.

In 2002, Jon Montgomery decided to start training for the first time in his life to compete in skeleton, a winter sledding sport. He practiced thousands of times down the same track until he got it perfect and knew every tweak needed to shave off the fraction of a second he needed to win gold. He qualified for the Vancouver 2010 Winter Olympics based on his results in the 2009–2010 Skeleton World Cup, and in Vancouver he won the gold medal.

He stood proudly on top of that podium in 2010 because he had a dream, a deep belief, an inner core feeling, and a relentless hunger to be the gold medal winner! He did it!

The same goes with running multiple businesses at the same time. I meet many business owners who are building multilevel marketing companies and/or sometimes one or two of their own businesses. My first question to them is, which one of these businesses makes you the money that you want? In most cases, the answer is, "None of them, but together I'm making some money." My advice in this case is to take one business and give it that laser focus, and you will watch how dramatically different your results will be. You'll start to see that as you focus on one thing, you'll give it more of your energy, since your effort will no longer be diluted between many different activities in multiple businesses.

Once you've made your first business successful, I would recommend hiring a president to run the business for you so that you can go out and build your next entrepreneurial initiative, or sell it for a good price. My definition of a successful business is one that pays you what you want, gives you the time off that you want, and allows you to live the lifestyle that you want. So before you start your next business, ensure that the first business is giving you all three of those criteria.

The biggest cause of failure for most entrepreneurs are the bright, shiny objects that distract you continuously and leave you unfocused. You are an entrepreneur; you love being creative and implementing new ideas. The sad part is that without focus, you will never get where you want to be. I am not saying all ideas are bad and should not be implemented, it's just a matter of determining whether or not they will enhance your business and get you faster to your goal. It's also called the "crow syndrome," or continuously bouncing around from bright, shiny item to bright, shiny item, just like a crow.

At our office we have a "parking lot" where we write down all the ideas that we want to implement, and twice a year we look at the parking lot and decide what needs to be done. Some items stay on the parking lot for a while, and others are implemented during these strategic planning sessions. What I find interesting is how many items on the parking lot were very exciting at the time and we thought would be awesome to implement, and a few months later we looked at them and decided that they were not that important, and even that they would be costly and erode our bottom line.

I cannot stress enough how much focus can impact your results. Of course, you need a vivid vision and a plan in order to have something to focus on.

BE TENACIOUS, DRIVEN, AND CONVICTED

SUCCESS SPOTLIGHT!

The more people you meet, the quicker you will get your name out there and grow your business.

I find that many business owners do not have the staying power or tenacity to build a successful business and avoid those bright, shiny objects. What you need to do today is to take what you have and complete the dream. Before you started the business, you had a vision for where you wanted to go, and until you get there, you have not succeeded. Being tenacious is one of the most important things an entrepreneur can learn, as this will keep you hungry, focused, and on the dynamic path to success.

When I first started out with my training and consulting company, I knew it would take time to build my reputation in the seminar industry, so I ensured that the Pro CEO Consulting business was extremely healthy and could financially assist the seminar side of the company. Initially I did events where there were only three or four people in the room. This continued for close to six months, as our name got out into the marketplace via those few people, we started to achieve our financial goals, and we were able to afford to hire people to assist us in the business. Now our business is highly focused on the seminars. I still do Pro CEO Consulting, and I now have the luxury to choose the clients I work with and assist them with achieving extreme results in their businesses.

Most business owners do not have the tenacity to continue this month after month for six months. The reason why I was able to continue is that I had a vivid vision for where I was going, I had laser focus, and I had a detailed one-page business plan for the path on how to get there.

Your mind will play many games with you and will often want to take you out of the game. Being in control of your mind and being aware that your mind wants to take you out of the game is really important. Your mind is designed to keep you safe at all times. This includes assisting you with excuses and justifying why you should deviate from your plan or even give up. Tenacity is vital to knowing what you need to do and going out and doing it.

In the beginning days of Make Your Mark, we attended twelve to sixteen networking events a week. Yes, a week! Getting your business going is a simple formula; the more people you meet, the quicker you will get your name out there and grow your business. It took a ton of effort to go out and network every day, yet I knew it was what was required to get where I wanted to be. I had to force myself into the car, put a smile on my face, pump up my positive attitude, and go out and do it!

FOLLOW YOUR
OWN RULES

SUCCESS
SPOTLIGHT!

There are only two sets of rules in business: your rules and the customers' rules.

If clients are calling you at all hours,
they are in control of your business and life!

I also find that the success you achieve is directly related to how much structure you have in your business. The more rules and structure you have and adhere to, the more your customers respect you and the better your results. If you do not respect yourself by creating rules in your own life and business, why should a customer respect you? Often, if you have no rules, your customers make them for you, or you make them up on the fly, which causes long-term problems and challenges. This is where we end up with clients in our databases that we would love to fire—but it's not their fault we had no rules!

There are only *two* sets of rules in business: your rules and the customers' rules. You want to run your business according to your rules. Otherwise, you will have your clients making rules for you that you are not pleased with, and they will be truly in charge of your business.

Here are a few examples of the rules that you should have in your business to create the structure that you want:

- Core values
- Client rules (niche marketing)
- Pricing rules, which dictate the profit you want to make
- Discount rules

- Return policies
- Warranties and guarantees
- Office hours
- Communication response times
- Delivery times
- Emergency contact times and numbers
- Social media rules
- Client care policies
- Expense policies
- Gift policies
- Referral programs
- Loyalty programs

There are a lot more of these rules and structures that you can put in place, but the most important part is understanding that when you have rules in place, it lets your prospects and clients know that you have a structured business. At certain times you may have to deviate slightly from these rules, and you should either modify the rule you have or make an exception. Exceptions should be extremely rare. If you are often making exceptions, then you need to relook at the rules you have in place and adjust them accordingly.

Many rules are broken because the entrepreneur does not want to let their client down and feels compelled to win the order, or maybe does not want to upset the client or prospect. Deviating from your rules causes chaos and often ongoing expectations. And it only lets your client know that you can be manipulated into changing things to suit them. Once you let a client walk over you, they will continue to expect this and in some cases will drive you crazy!

If you are forever shifting the rules, you will cause chaos in your business, and you will be running according to rules that your clients make up for you. They will often bring their friends who expect the same, and you will end up with a database of clients you're serving for little to no income! Remember, you do have the right to fire clients. At our Sales Warrior event, we talk about *value* and finding and retaining clients. The most important skill you need to learn in sales is that "cost is only an issue in the absence of value," and that if you are dropping your price, you most likely do not understand your value. We have a specialized process called the value calculator that people learn at the Sales Warrior event to assist with determining value. Once you know your value, you will very seldom reduce your price.

We have lived by the headline, "Is finding more clients causing you stress?" But adding a single word makes it go hand-in-hand with value: "Is finding *profitable* clients causing you stress?"

I always say that clients are like children: when you have a well-structured environment, it leads them to respect you and understand that you are in control of where your business is going. If we have no rules for children, chaos prevails, and that's often what I see in many small businesses. Pricing varies from one client to another, discounts are not fixed, and clients can call them any time.

The most important part of setting rules is ensuring that you follow them. This demonstrates to your clients, colleagues, and staff that you know what you are doing.

You might say that you don't have rules in your business because you are small or a start-up and that it's not important, but in fact it's critical. The sooner you set the rules, the sooner you will find profitable and ideal clients. Sadly, many entrepreneurs break the rules because the order the client is holding is more than what is in the entrepreneur's bank account, so they drop their price and are completely abused by the client. Also, when you capitulate and drop your price, your client often goes out and tells others, and now you have a number of clients wanting the same service and/or product for the same prices. This is when you start limiting your success in your business!

There are some instances when you may alter the rules, and a good one is when you want to get a client onboard who will add a ton of credibility to your business and whom you know you can use in your marketing to generate more clients. The most important part is setting the rules for the deal, and also ensuring that the rules are extremely well communicated to the client.

I have trained for many large organizations like Sun Life Financial, Curves, Bank of Montreal, Bank of Nova Scotia, and Fitness Town, and I can tell you that I structured an outrageous offer to get Sun Life Financial onboard. I knew that once they were a client, I could use their name in meetings and proposals (with testimonials), and if they trusted me, it would add huge credibility to who I am and what I can deliver. Because of Sun Life Financial, I ended up winning the Bank of Montreal as a client at my full rate.

LEAD BY EXAMPLE

SUCCESS
SPOTLIGHT!
Leadership is very simple: complain up, and motivate and inspire downwards and sideways.

This leads me to the topic of leadership as an entrepreneur. I am not going to go too much into the details of what leadership means, other than to give you a few examples for you to fully understand and comprehend what it means to be a leader in your company.

Very simply put, leadership can be defined in one sentence, and I learned this from our chairman of the board of the metallurgical equipment company. He used to say to me, "Colin, it's very lonely at the top! You are at the top of this company, and the one piece of advice I can give you as the leader of this company is very simple: complain up, and motivate and inspire downwards and sideways." What this means is that if you have any challenging situations as a leader of your company, you should not take them to people who are your subordinates. It's your job to take on the challenges and lead and inspire those people to new heights of success. This is why it makes it so lonely when you're at the top, because you take all the complaints, but really at the end of the day you have nobody to complain to.

If you complain to your team about any other member of the team, it conveys the message that it's acceptable to behave in this fashion, and you will create a negative virus or culture in your company.

Another important part of being the leader in your business is to understand that all the systems, processes, and structures that you put in place need to be followed precisely. If you do not follow what you have put in place, nobody else in your business will follow either. As the leader of your company, everybody watches everything that you do, and whatever you do gives them permission to do the same. Very simply put, if you have a gift policy in place that says you do not spend more than $50 per client on a gift, and you as the owner go out and spend $100 on a client, it gives your team the understanding that the $50 gift rule is truly not a rule.

Similarly, if you want your staff to show up to meetings on time, you have to be on time as well—whatever you do, your staff and clients will follow! Yes, you can say that you are the boss and that they should do what they are told, but you will not gain respect this way. The most important leadership principle to follow is that you lead by example, by doing exactly what you expect from your clients, staff, and colleagues.

PLAN TO SACRIFICE

SUCCESS
SPOTLIGHT!
Are you doing business or playing business?

This is probably the most alarming area for me that I see with many entrepreneurs. In order to grow a very successful business, you need to make sacrifices to get there. Especially in the beginning, when you're first starting out, a lot of sacrifices need to be made so that you can follow your plan and hit your goals for your first year. The sad part is so many business owners just do not have a written plan, and they spend many hours running around thinking that they are really doing business, while they are only really playing business.

I understand that you start a business to give you the flexibility to work when you want and do what you want. To be honest, this only starts once you have crossed the initial success finish line! If you decide from the day you start to do non-business-building activities during office hours, like going for lunch, making personal calls, taking long vacations on credit cards, having coffee with buddies, or watching TV, then you will take a long time to achieve the results you want! I watch people at networking events who say they are there to build their business, and two years or so down the line they are still in the same place in terms of success and financial stability. The biggest reason is that they do not have a sacrifice plan.

According to the US Department of Labor's Bureau of Labor Statistics, the average man spends 38.99 hours per week in leisure activities, and the average woman 33.74 hours. According to the report, those leisure activities are divided up into three key activities: TV watching; video gaming; and using a computer for leisure, socializing, and communicating.

This equates to doing these activities three to four hours per day, every single day of the week. These three key leisure activities can do very little to build your business. If you just took half the number of leisure hours per month and put them toward your business, you would have sixty hours per month more to build a very successful business. What would sixty hours a month do for your business currently? I'm sure it would be the difference between a super-successful business in the next twelve months and a business with limited results, especially when you are in the start-up phase of your business.

Once your business gets to a level of success and has gained a certain amount of momentum in the marketplace, you can certainly reduce the amount of sacrifice that you have to make by bringing in key staff to help you and assist you in running your business.

The most important decision that you have to make is: are you prepared to make the sacrifices in order to achieve the results that you are after? Part of your planning is to plan how long you will make the sacrifices for in order to achieve the goals you want in the next three, six, and twelve months!

When I start a business or decide to take my business to the next level, I put together a sacrifice plan for a set period of time. I let my family know that I am in start-up or build phase, and that for the next six months, I will be highly focused on achieving results according to my one-page business plan. I sit down with my wife and two daughters and let them know why I am doing it and to check in with me on a certain date to hold me accountable to my sacrifice plan. I do not sacrifice all my time with my family. I do plan a date night a week with my wife and an evening with my kids, but outside of that, I am in build mode and will do whatever it takes to get where I need to be.

At the end of the six months, we sit down as a family and re-evaluate where we are at and how things have gone. What this does is communicate with your family about what your plans are and where you want to be, and fully involves them in your business. I often have a family reward at the end of the sacrifice plan where we go and do something as a family—a trip to Disneyland, Mexico, a show, etc. Choose something that is important to your family, and they will assist you on your path to massive success.

MANAGE YOUR COMMITMENTS,
NOT YOUR TIME

SUCCESS
SPOTLIGHT!
There is no such thing as time management... It's all about managing your commitments.

Are you like most of the business owners and entrepreneurs in the marketplace who don't have enough hours in the day? I can tell you that of the thousands of business owners I have met, the majority of them do not have a time management issue. They have a commitment management issue.

What I mean by this is that you cannot truly manage time, as there are only a set number of seconds, minutes, and hours in a day. What you can truly manage are all the commitments that you make—not only to yourself, but to other people as well. Commitment management goes hand-in-hand with the rules that you set up in your business. When you're first starting out in your business, you seem to run around like a headless chicken because you're always chasing the order, but really at the end of the day you're truly chasing the money.

A prospect only has to call and say that they are interested in your product or service, and you will drop everything to go and see them. But most of the time, if you have not done your homework properly, you come home empty handed. It is not how quickly you rush out to the meeting that is important, it is how quickly you prepare and get yourself organized to wow the prospect and give them a solution they are looking for with a product or service that you have to offer—that is what's important!

One of the most important commitments is the one to yourself. When you set time aside to be in your office working on your business, then do not let a prospect or client pull you away from what you have committed to doing for your business. I find this one of the weakest areas for entrepreneurs, as we are always chasing the sale and will drop some of the most important business-building activities to sometimes go out and see a "hot lead," when really it's not that hot, and all that ends up happening is you waste your most valuable time.

Part of this is also learning to say *no* more frequently. If you have an appointment booked with yourself, then treat it as if it were an appointment with a client. Should another client call, say "no" if it's going to impact your commitments to yourself, and simply book another time with them when you are available. If you truly did have another appointment booked with a client, you would not be able to make the appointment anyway. Do this, and you will start to feel like you are truly in control of your business and all your commitments.

I personally sit down every Sunday evening and look at the activities that I have for the week, whether it be

Business or Life Seminars, Pro CEO Consulting, BEST Mindset Groups, KAP-IT Success Groups, keynote meetings, client meetings, going to the gym, cycling, family time, leisure time, etc. I then take my calendar and fill out all the commitments that I have for the week. The remaining time in between those commitments is the time that I have available to complete all the other activities on my to-do list. When you do this for your business on a weekly basis, some weeks you will see that your to-do list often has many more things on it than the time that you have available, outside of the commitments that you already have.

The next thing that you need to do is understand how to prioritize your to-do list, because there are often more to-do items than there is available time. So you need to decide what activities absolutely must be done that week and what can wait until the following week. It is important to do this, because it does take a ton of stress out of your business and day, as you're not running out of time each day because you have planned your time around the commitments that you have.

In fact, in my own business I do not have meetings with people unless there is an agenda for the meeting. Even if it is a thirty-minute meeting for a cup of coffee with a student, I always ask for a simple agenda by e-mail to know what they want to talk about, because this does three things: first, it allows us to cover the topic effectively in the time available; second, we get to the point quicker; and third, it shortens the meeting and honors each other's time.

There are lots of entrepreneurs and prospects out in the marketplace that will easily occupy all your time if you allow them. They will want to meet to discuss using your services or products or even joint venturing together. Plus, there are lots of people out there with amazing opportunities and things that they want to sell you, which are often bright, shiny objects. Do not get sidetracked by something that is going to take you off track and away from your goals that you have set for yourself. Be very careful of bright, shiny objects, and stay true to your goals and dreams!

HUNGER FOR SUCCESS;
DON'T JUST WISH FOR IT

SUCCESS
SPOTLIGHT!
If you are hungry for success, you will find ways to make things work! It's that simple!

Most entrepreneurs have a desire to achieve huge success, but they are often hampered by their thinking or are easily taken out of the game by outside influences. Desire is something that is nostalgic or a feeling you have when you think about something. You desire it, it would be nice to have, but are you truly hungry for it?

Hunger takes desire to an entirely new level. When you hunger to achieve a goal, it can be felt to your inner core and you will do whatever it takes to achieve the goal.

You will not let things stand in your way!

I get asked frequently, "How do you develop a hunger for what you do?" The crucial item to have in place is a plan that includes income, profit, and sacrifices. Until you have a set plan, you can only have a desire, because you have no plan to achieve the goal you want. Once you have the plan in place, it takes a massive belief in yourself, laser focus, and dedication to implement it and cross the finish line without getting distracted.

You can have the desire for a nice, new home with all the bells and whistles, but until you write down on paper what it's going to take to achieve the desired result, you will have no daily, weekly, or monthly action plan in place that tells you what must be done in order to get there. You need a plan, just like the Olympic athlete discussed earlier. His plan was to stand on the podium to receive a gold medal, so he found the right mentors and coaches, and then divided up his activities into what he had to do month-by-month in order to qualify each year to even be considered for selection to the Canadian Olympic team. He started with the end in mind and then knew what he had to do on a quarterly, monthly, weekly, and daily basis in order to achieve the result! If you want to have a million-dollar business in twelve months' time, you will have to work it back to where you are today in order to give you the laser focus and a detailed action plan, starting now!

Hunger takes into account everything we have discussed in the first part of the book. I have a little fun with the students at our events and tell them that I am going to a two-hour networking event in Vancouver between 11 p.m. and 1 a.m. that has three hundred people in attendance who are high quality and will provide a great opportunity for them. I then ask the question, "Who is coming with me?" It is really interesting to hear the responses. Here are the typical ones:

- I am there for sure.
- Please give me all the details first.
- I am too tired.
- I have a busy day tomorrow.
- I have family commitments.
- Let me check with my spouse.

…And the list goes on!

If you are *hungry*, you will find a way to make things work! It's that simple! True entrepreneurs are solution driven and not hindered by hurdles. They will find a way to make it over the hurdle, and if another hurdle comes up, they will find the next solution and keep going!

You will even do things that you do not like doing, such as getting up early. You may hear yourself say, "I don't like getting up early, and it takes me a while to get going in the morning," or "I am not a morning person!" Guess what, if you keep on reinforcing this statement, you will never like getting up early and may miss tons of opportunities.

My question to you is, what would have been your response to the above question? Would you come with me, or do you find yourself using one of the key excuses above— or do you have your own arsenal of excuses?

When you have *hunger*, you seldom have any *excuses*, or *reasons* why you cannot do something to build your business! You evaluate and take decisive action!

DELIVER RESULTS,
NOT EXCUSES

SUCCESS
SPOTLIGHT!
There are only results or excuses!

To continue from the previous topic, there really are only two drivers in whether you achieve your goals: results or excuses.

Some people are even talented enough at making excuses to have a pre-excuse before the actual excuse. When you want enhanced results from your business, you have to cut out the excuses and realize that there is no middle ground; it's either results or excuses.

What do you want in your business?

If it's results you are after, then you have to eliminate the excuses from your daily activities. I hear thousands of excuses of why things cannot be done, and here are a few of the key ones:

- I am too tired.
- I have worked hard this week and deserve some time off.
- I just feel like staying at home with my family tonight.
- They will have another event next week or soon.
- Seven a.m. is too early to be at a meeting.
- I like to sleep in and start meetings at 10 a.m.
- I am not fully prepared yet.

Excuses are manmade reasons and hurdles that we place in front of ourselves, whether consciously or subconsciously, that constantly hold us back from achieving amazing success.

Listen to yourself on a daily basis and be fully self-aware of the *excuses* you are using that stop you from getting things done.

Another item that goes hand-in-hand with excuses, is a partner in crime with procrastination, and holds people back from achieving great results quickly is the word *when*. This word often keeps people from taking action and achieving results quickly. Here are a few examples of common "when" statements:

- When I have business cards, I will go networking.
- When my website is live, I will…
- When my partner does ABC, I will do…
- When I have the money, I will take risks.
- When I can afford to, I will invest in…

When, when, when, when…just do it!

There are a ton more "when" statements that I am sure you have heard, and all they are doing is stopping you from going out and achieving results. There are always solutions to the above problems and hurdles that we put before ourselves; all you have to do is create the solution and do it. Do not let "when" hold you back from getting things done!

BE SOLUTION DRIVEN

SUCCESS SPOTLIGHT!

Attitude is everything!

The best way to illustrate this is with a very powerful example.

I was recently training at our two-day Sales Warrior seminar and had two realtors in the audience of forty. We gave them an exercise to go out and sell a spa music CD that belonged to one of my previous companies. One of the realtors approached me immediately and said to me how stupid the idea was and that she was not going to do it. The other realtor did not say a word and took a handful of CDs off the table and went on his way to sell CDs during the lunch break. Upon returning from the lunch break, the first realtor was still pretty upset by the task that had been asked of her. She sat down in her chair, and before I could even get the room under control for the afternoon session, her hand went up immediately and she told me how stupid the exercise was.

Another student from the back of the room put up her hand and asked if she could ask a question, to which I said, "Absolutely!" She said to the realtor, "Why do you not want to sell the CDs?" The realtor immediately replied without hesitation that she cannot sell something that she has not heard or that she is not passionate about! The other student asked the realtor another question, and said, "Did you drive your vehicle to the event today?" Her reply was, "Of course I did!" She said to her, "Why did you not open the CD and play it in your car during the lunch break? Then you would have been able to listen to the music, and it would've been easy to sell it." The immediate response to this was, "I could've done that, but then how would I be able to sell a product that has been opened?"

I often see and hear entrepreneurs and business owners place huge hurdles in front of themselves, and as you take them out of their way, they will place another hurdle before themselves, rather than taking action and experiencing the journey. How often do you see yourself in similar situations, placing hurdles before yourself on an ongoing basis? You can always find reasons why not to do something, because it keeps you comfortable and doing the same things—and of course achieving the same results! You must realize that the knowledge that got you to where you are today is not the knowledge that will get you to where you want to be! Plus, to achieve what you have never achieved, you have to do things that you have never done!

Once this conversation was over, the other realtor got up and said that he had sold sixty-seven CDs during the lunch break. The entire class was given the exact same exercise to do, and the only difference between one achieving outrageous success and the other achieving none was purely mindset, which directly impacts your attitude and the results that you will achieve. This exercise is not a sales exercise—it's a brain-chatter exercise to see what noise happens between your ears when you are asked to do something that is completely out of your comfort zone!

The lady realtor had the biggest aha moment at this event and has since gone from the top 5 percent of realtors in her area to the top 1 percent!

DO NOT LISTEN TO THE
WRONG PEOPLE

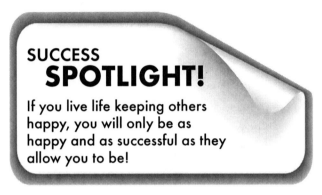

SUCCESS
SPOTLIGHT!
If you live life keeping others happy, you will only be as happy and as successful as they allow you to be!

This is probably my favorite topic in this entire section, because I cannot understand why people take advice from people who have no expertise in the given area of business or entrepreneurship. Most business owners listen to their spouses who have never run a business, never intend to run a business, and most of the time have zero education or understanding of what it's like to be an entrepreneur or a business owner.

I often say to our students that you would not go to the plumber to get a haircut, or ask a hairdresser to come and do your electrical work in your home. Yet people do this every single day as entrepreneurs and business owners. If you take advice from anybody, my biggest piece of advice for you is to find people who are extremely successful at what you are looking for advice in, and ask them to assist you!

I cannot stress this enough as you go out and build your business. The first question you should be asking anybody who is giving you advice, or even thinking in your mind, is, "Should I be listening to this person?"

In my personal life, I use the same strategy. When I go to an investment advisor, and they give me advice on what to invest in, my first question to them is, "Do you have your own money invested in the same investment strategy?" If not, I'll ask them why—and why would they be putting my money where their money is not?

The same goes for when you're listening to your customers or prospects. If they are giving you marketing advice, or are disgruntled with an e-mail that you sent out to your entire database, ask yourself if you should be listening to that person. In the marketing world, we have a statement that goes as follows: "When you're focused on the foxes, don't be listening to the yapping hounds." When you send out an e-mail to your database, there will always be people who will have something to say about what you sent out. If it is only one or two e-mails, then do not let them dictate the way you do your marketing. Just hit delete and forget about it and go focus on the people who responded in a positive light.

Never change your focus, structure, rules, or anything in your business because one person said you should change it, unless you believe it is important to change. The most important thing to understand is that you should listen to your customers and colleagues, but do not change your entire business every time one of them gives you a comment or a suggestion. If you make changes every single time they give you a comment or a suggestion, they are truly in control of your business and setting the rules for you, and this is not what you want.

Like I said earlier, our office has what we call a "parking lot" for new ideas and suggestions. Twice a year we look at all the ideas and suggestions on the parking lot and decide if we are going to implement them, change them, or just keep them the way they are. This is a decision that we make and implement accordingly.

I have attended many networking groups over the past decades, and I can tell you that these groups can dramatically impact your business, both positively and negatively. I have found groups where people hang out for months and sometimes years, and you see them in exactly the same place they were a few years back. This is not totally the group's fault at all, but I can tell you the people you associate with will impact the success of your business. If you want to be a million-dollar business, then pay the fees to belong to a group where million-dollar business owners hang out. Similarly, if you are a start-up, go to groups where there are successful start-up businesses.

I have seen groups that sometimes go as far as supporting each other even though they are not successful. They hang out together and bond rather than go out and find groups that will inspire them and take them to new heights! Ask yourself, "Why do I belong to this group?" If you are not getting the results you want, then make a change. I understand that you may say it's because there are great people in the group and that you like seeing them on a regular basis. You have to remember that you are networking to grow your business significantly and not to validate your own poor performance by hanging out with other poor performers. Be very careful of this! Your time is valuable and should be used to maximize the growth of your business.

I started two business groups as part of Make Your Mark: BEST Mindset and KAP-IT Success Groups. Neither of them are networking groups—they are designed for start-up entrepreneurs to seasoned veterans in business and are discussed at the end of the book!

It's really this simple: do not change your business, marketing, sales, or strategic decisions for people who are not going to buy from you anyway. I see entrepreneurs change the content of an e-mail because their spouse found it too hard hitting, when their spouse is not even a potential buyer of the product or service. In the marketing world, we say, "Never dilute your sales copy to not offend somebody who is not your customer!"

Be extremely careful to who you listen to, and surround yourself with people who are experts in the area that you are looking for advice in!

TAKE ADVICE FROM
SUCCESSFUL PEOPLE

SUCCESS
SPOTLIGHT!
Listen to successful people
and do exactly what they say.

Now that you understand that your entrepreneurial and financial success will directly reflect the kinds of people you allow to speak into your life, the critical part is taking *action* on the advice that you have been given.

A friend and business colleague, Dwayne Stewart, was presenting at our Business Excellence seminar (a three-day event), and spoke about how "hope is not a strategy." He has a very detailed step-by-step manual on how to build a successful construction company from the ground up, just like the one that he owns and operates. He said that most business owners are so scared that their staff will run off with the manual and start their own business. Instead of worrying about this, Dwayne simply says, "You can give people every minute ounce of detail, and they will still decide that the process needs fixing or improvement along the way and end up failing!"

The biggest frustration for me in our seminars is that we teach cutting-edge business trainings, solutions, and systems, and many of the students you meet months down the line are still doing things exactly the way they did before they walked into the trainings. They get all the advice in the world and do not implement what they have learned.

In my Pro CEO Consulting practice, the first thing I evaluate before working with a client is how open they are to receiving advice, processing it, and implementing it exactly. I have worked with some business owners over the past twenty years who beg you to assist them, and when you give them advice, they go off and do something completely different. Or they go from person to person getting advice and doing nothing with the advice other than comparing what one person said versus the other, and even sometimes being critical about the advice that people are giving!

When I was writing this book, I was working with seven Pro CEO Consulting clients, and the one achieving the most rapid results was the owner of a business called Mr. Cover All. This company sells awnings, roll screens, and roller shutters for your patio and store fronts. Now, being in Vancouver, Canada, we only have around four months per year of great outdoor weather. The owner of Mr. Cover All came to me and said that the business has very slow months from December to March, great months between April and August, and average months between September and November. I looked at their structure and systems and started working with them in January (the slowest month of the year).

On average this company had very low revenues and profit in the slow months, about double the revenues in the summer months, and about 50 percent revenues in the average months. By the end of January, they were already earning the revenues they typically did in the summer months, and by the strong summer months, sales increased six fold—just by changing the way they did things in the company regarding exposure, sales, operations, and marketing.

Every bit of advice I gave was implemented exactly the way that I presented it to them!

You can go and ask for all the advice in the world, and when it comes from people who are substantially more successful in those areas than you are, just listen, take notes, and do exactly what they say! Not only will it make you tons of money, it will save you tons as well! Plus, it will give you the time off you want!

FOCUS ON REWARDS,
NOT PENALTIES!

SUCCESS
SPOTLIGHT!
What you focus on,
shows up in your life!

In life, realize that no matter what you say out loud or in your mind, it shows up! I have spent time with thousands of business owners over the past twenty years, and it stuns me how many people will go to the bank and get credit to fund their business through lines of credit, remortgaging, or credit cards, and be totally focused on the *penalty* rather than the *reward* of the money they have just received.

If you decide to add more debt to your life or business, focus on what you want it to bring you. I hear comments like, "What happens if I add this last $20,000 from my equity in my home to my business and I lose it, or my business fails?" For most, I see them lose it, and their business fails because they are totally focused on the penalty, rather than the reward of what the $20,000 is going to do or bring them in their business. What they are focused on shows up!

What happens if we turned the focus toward the reward of how the $20,000 will allow you to take your business to new heights and will give you the freedom to hire a new person and dramatically grow your sales and profitability? Does this sound different? For sure it does. Then why are we so focused on the negative? I can tell you why: most people do not have a twelve-month Cash Flow Predictor™ plan that will assist them in planning their business and understanding what a cash investment could do for their success. (See chapter 5 for more about the Cash Flow Predictor plan.) When you have a cash flow plan (taught at our Profit Warrior Event), it allows you to know:

- What cash flow is and how to manage it like the wealthy
- HOW, WHEN, and WHY to find financing for your business long before you need it
- How to truly understand all aspects of PROFITABILITY in your business
- WHAT key items to keep control of to ensure you become and maintain your profitability
- HOW to make key financial decisions with minimal impact on your business
- How to work with your VENDORS to benefit your business and cash flow
- How to accurately determine your break-even point and what each dollar spent truly costs you
- How to keep an eye on your dollars to ensure you know what your bookkeeper and accountant are doing
- How to stop financial disaster in your business and smooth out the HUGE economic swings

Are you focused on the rewards or the penalties of your business dealings?

The universe does not know right from wrong, and it will only deliver what you are asking for! So, if you decide to add more money to your business, decide what it is going to be for in terms of the growth and rewards before you get it.

If you worry about what it's going to do for your business, you are focusing on the penalty, and the universe will only give you what you focus on! So examine the thoughts and words that you use. Decide today: "Am I focused on the rewards of what I am doing, or the penalty?"

BE PASSIONATE ABOUT
WHAT YOU ARE DOING

SUCCESS
SPOTLIGHT!
When you are passionate and you stay focused on the true intentions of your business, the money will come easily.

I get asked quite frequently: how do you know if you're passionate about what you're doing? I used to find this a tough question to answer, and then I came up with a very simple question to ask that would assist a person quickly determine if they are passionate about what they're doing. "If you were earning $10,000 per month and I could pay you that $10,000, would you keep doing what you're doing or would you do something else?" If the answer to this question is yes, you would keep on doing it even if you had to do it for free, then you're most definitely passionate about what you do. If you answered no to the question, and said that you would rather be doing something else, then the chances of you being passionate about what you are doing currently is just about zero. If you're not passionate about what you do, decide to make the change today. When you are passionate and you stay focused on the true intentions of your business, the money will come easily.

This may be a tough decision for you, but I can tell you that if you're struggling in your business financially and wondering why you're struggling, it may have something to do with your passion for what you are doing.

I know every day that I'm living my passion, because I jump out of bed with a bounce in my step, knowing that I'm going out to change the lives of business owners, entrepreneurs, and their families.

DO NOT OVERSERVICE
YOUR CLIENTS!

SUCCESS
SPOTLIGHT!
A disgruntled client is only truly satisfied when he buys from you again!

This is one of the most overlooked topics when you're first starting a business and going out on the entrepreneurial path to success. When you first start out, you may not have that many prospects or clients, so it is very easy to quickly communicate back and forth with them in very short periods of time—sometimes instantaneously, or within a few minutes, or maybe an hour or two. The challenging part is that as you grow your business and you have more inquiries coming in and more responses to get back to, it becomes difficult to maintain what you initially started with your first group of clients.

What I recommend when you start up a company is that you do not overservice your clients in the beginning. Let your clients know that you will get back to them within twenty-four hours, whether they communicate to you via e-mail, Facebook, fax, etc. This lets them know that you have rules in your business, and it also gives the impression that you are busy and that you have other clients to respond to. If you are too hungry sometimes and respond very quickly, it often conveys the message to the customer that you are a starving business owner and may even convey desperation.

It does also prevent you from having clients come back to you, as you grow and get busier, and say that you are no longer looking after their needs and that your response times have dramatically increased. Clients can be very sensitive to this and sometimes take things very personally when your response times change.

Set the rules in the beginning around response times, and you will always be in a great position as your business grows to huge levels of success.

RELENTLESS FOLLOW-UP
AND FOLLOW THROUGH

SUCCESS
SPOTLIGHT!
Keep in contact until you
get a yes or no answer.

The acronym for *follow-up* is F.U.! This is what you tell your prospects or clients every time you say you are going to follow up, and you do not. Or when you go out to networking events, trade shows, or any public venue where you collect people's business cards and details, and then weeks later you have not followed up, or sometimes you cannot even remember where you met them. Most of all, you cannot remember a thing about them (not to mention that most business cards are so vague about what people do that you cannot figure out anything about them).

Here is what makes people who are doing business seriously stand out from those who are playing business:

1. Setting time aside for follow-up. When you are planning your weekly agenda and you know you are going out to public events, cocktail parties, business gatherings, or official networking events,

ensure that you set time aside later in the day or the next day to complete the follow-up. The follow-up is more important than the event itself. At Exposure Warrior, we teach companies how to effectively network and make significant money. Your intention when you go networking is to grow your business, which really means to make money! Yes, it's acceptable to say this! The relationships you attract during networking events and the results you achieve will be directly proportional to the energy you put out there towards your intention of attending the networking meeting.

2. When you go out networking, collect business cards and connect with people. The first thing I do after the event is write on the back of the card where I met the person (the event), the date, and what personal information I learned about them (how many kids, what ages, married, single, likes, dislikes, etc.).

3. I also write on the back of the card what I gave them: business card, brochure, flyer, sample, offer, everything, so that I do not forget. If they do not have a business card, or their business card has graphics on the back and no space to write, have a little note pad available to take detailed notes and staple them to their card.

4. Immediately (later that day or maximum twenty-four hours later) after the event I e-mail all the people I met *separately* as individuals, not mass

e-mails. In the e-mails I write to them, I talk about some of the personal connection items we had and set up a time to meet with them at a future date to discuss business or any other opportunities.

5. If I gave them a flyer for an upcoming event, I have my office staff follow up within twenty-four hours to ensure that the person knows the details and that we get them confirmed for the event. You can do this as it relates to the products or services you have to offer.

6. If you want the business, you had better be doing the follow-up.

7. How much is too much? Here are the most common excuses for not doing effective follow-up:

    a. I do not want to seem like I am stalking them.

    b. I have phoned and e-mailed and they have not replied, so they are obviously not interested.

    c. If they want my product or service, they will call me! If you have the latest and greatest toy, maybe this will happen. Otherwise, you will get really old waiting for the call! They are the prospective client, and it's your job to chase them without being invasive.

    d. I do not want to be bugging them.

    e. They won't remember who I am.

The list of excuses goes on and on for not doing effective follow-up. Most of the above are just your mind taking you out of the game! The only reason why you are even coming up with these excuses is because you have not built a strong relationship with the prospect or client. When you have strong relationships that are genuine, and you have the best intention when you phone, 99 percent of the time you'll receive a great response.

Just fricking do it!

The simple formula is that you keep in contact until you get a YES or NO answer from them.

And when you get a NO, it means NO for now, not in the future. Keep following up and never stop!

8. It's very simple: the relentless and tenacious business owner who FOLLOWS UP, stays focused on the task of winning, and eliminates excuses is the one who WINS hugely in business.

Are you relentless or full of excuses?

Example: A friend and colleague wanted the graphic design and print contract for a large coffee chain, and called the VP of Marketing every month for four-and-a-half years. He won the contract eventually in January 2010, and it's been massive for his business. Work it out: he called over fifty times to the same person, and all he would say is, "How are things, and can I assist you in any way?" They said NO over fifty times, and in January 2010, they said, "We have a problem with our existing supplier; come in and see us," and the rest is history!

How tenacious are you?

Are you prepared to go the extra thousand miles with your follow-up, or are you going to keep doing it the same way expecting a different result? Start implementing the key follow-up points above, and watch your business change and profits soar!

If you keep doing poor follow-up, you are truly telling your client F.U.!

There are very effective ways for doing follow-up, from having a manual card system to a fully integrated computer system that manages your leads, like a client relationship management system (or CRM, as it's commonly called). It really does not matter how you do it, just so long as you have a system, you follow it, and you get the follow-up done in order to achieve the results you are after. I can tell you that by increasing your follow-up effectiveness, you will dramatically improve client relationships and sales in your business!

Here are some sales statistics that will get you really thinking:

- 48 percent of salespeople never follow up with a prospect.
- 25 percent of salespeople make a second contact and stop.
- 12 percent of salespeople only make a third contact and stop.
- ONLY 10 percent of salespeople make more than three contacts.

- 2 percent of sales are made on the first contact.
- 3 percent of sales are made on the second contact.
- 5 percent of sales are made on the third contact.
- 10 percent of sales are made on the fourth contact.
- 80 percent of sales are made on the fifth through twelfth contact!

The above statistics tell you how important follow-up is to your business! You can go out and do all the networking, attend all the business meetings, and gather as many business cards as you want, but without effective follow-up you are wasting your time, energy, and money!

UNDERSTAND THAT ENERGY
IS EVERYTHING!

SUCCESS
SPOTLIGHT!
Always show up with a winning and giving attitude, or don't leave your home or office!

I am amazed almost daily at how many business owners complain about their financial situation, and how things are really tough and not getting any better—yet they are not making any huge changes in habits or attitudes, or even making sacrifices to achieve what they want!

I suppose the number-one factor causing this is that most business owners are so focused on the mighty dollar and keeping their heads above water that they really do not have goals that they are focused on. Yes, they are operating from fear and anxiety rather than from a place of calmness and laser focus.

And to be truly honest, most business owners do not know what they WANT!

It really frustrates me and drives me crazy when business owners do not realize what they are saying and are not prepared to listen. Some even completely disregard the advice that you give because they believe that they know better. Why ask for the advice if you are not going to take it, use it, and profit from it?

Plus, they have the audacity to ask you to refer them or joint venture with them. I wish people would just remember that they have one mouth and two ears and that listening is important—doubly important!

I would say the number-two factor is that old, comfortable habits die hard, and some people do not realize that their poor habits, addictions, attitudes, and actions create a perception that can cause a person to not do business with them!

It's really as simple as saying you are going to show up for a free event or a networking group, and then just not showing up or informing people that you are not coming (just a little bit of common courtesy…please).

These ACTIONS SPEAK LOUDLY to the way you respect people and will most likely never have them referring you, because they may assume that that is how you always are—unpredictable and disrespectful!

To round this all off, all I can say is be aware of how and what you do in the public eye as it creates a perception in the eyes of others (which is their reality) and can and will cost you dearly!

Always show up with a winning and giving attitude, or don't leave your home or office! Remember, the one with the highest energy and superstar attitude almost always WINS!

HIRE THE RIGHT
RESOURCES

SUCCESS
SPOTLIGHT!

Anyone in your business who is in contact with your clients must have a client-care personality.

As your business grows, you are going to require additional people to assist you. The most important thing to remember, whether you are hiring part-time or full-time assistance, is to ensure that you have written down a detailed job description of what you expect them to do and deliver as part of their duties.

The second important item to consider is the following: anyone you have in contact with your prospects or clients, whether they are in accounting, shipping, sales, or marketing, must be part of your culture and have a client-care personality.

A third aspect to consider in the hiring process is the education, personality, and trainability of the employee. I frequently say that the education of the people who work for you is important, but the two most important characteristics I look for when hiring somebody is high likability (especially if they are dealing with clients) and trainability. I have found that it is easier to teach and educate your staff about your product or service than it is to teach them personality.

The fourth item is understanding that you hire people for what they are good at! You do not have to become best friends with them or socialize outside of office hours with them. You might find someone who is extremely good at what they do, and you may not necessarily like them, or they may not be your cup of tea as a friend, but you are hiring to grow your business, not to increase your circle of friends.

There are many books written on this topic of human resource management, and I want you to understand that the above items are what I live by at Make Your Mark.

PART THREE

THE INSTRUCTIONS

CHAPTER 6

DEVELOPING INTO A MASSIVELY SUCCESSFUL ENTREPRENEUR: FIFTEEN THINGS YOU MUST DO AFTER **READING THIS BOOK**

Just as we said in the beginning, preparing your workstation (developing a successful entrepreneurial mindset) and having all your ingredients at hand (understanding the nineteen crucial ingredients to entrepreneurial success) isn't enough. It's time to get cooking! Here are the fifteen things you must do immediately after reading this book to really turn your knowledge into profit.

COMPLETE YOUR ONE-PAGE BUSINESS PLAN AND
FIVE-YEAR VISION

SUCCESS
SPOTLIGHT!
Plan to win.

This is number one for a reason, because without a plan and vision you are truly going nowhere. You can download the one-page plan documents at www.My1PagePlan.com. Get this done as soon as you can!

COMPLETE YOUR CASH FLOW PREDICTOR™
FOR TWELVE MONTHS

SUCCESS
SPOTLIGHT!
Financial planning is vital to your business' well-being.

This is a very important document for your business and can be found in the same place: www.My1PagePlan.com. It is very simple to complete, and should you have any questions, we cover the full details at our Profit Warrior course. It will allow you to project out the next twelve months in your business and give you an understanding of where you are going and when you may need financing. As you make key decisions, you will use the document to see how it impacts your business.

KNOW YOUR FINANCIAL RISKS
AND GROSS MARGIN

SUCCESS
SPOTLIGHT!
You pay your expenses from gross profit, not revenue.

Starting a business does take a lot of courage, risk, determination, and tenacity to be successful. Yet the most neglected part of starting a business is the cash planning and knowing what money is required in order to grow and prosper. This must be done BEFORE you even start your business in order to determine if your business idea or concept is even financially viable with the model that you have created. Once you have downloaded the Cash Flow Predictor and tailored it for your business, you will start to realize what finances you have to have in place in order to achieve the success you want. Plus, it assists you with doing scenarios around your pricing, costs, and expenses to determine what is required if things do not go so well, or what kind of resources you are going to require when your business explodes with success, as well as the associated costs.

Many business owners do not understand basic accounting, and I am going to take you through the most important number to understand—your gross margin percentage. It allows us to calculate breakeven for everything you do in your business.

Here is a very simplified example:

At Make Your Mark, we sell Big Dreams, Gratitude, Successes, and Happiness Journals for $15, and they cost us $5. That means for every journal we sell we have a gross margin of $10, or $10 of profit before other expenses like salaries, office costs, etc. The gross margin percentage would also be $10/$15, or 66.67 percent. Simply understood, for every journal we sell, we only make $15 x 0.6667, or $10 of profit.

Let's say that this gross margin percentage, 66.67 percent, was the average for everything we do at Make Your Mark. This means that for every dollar we invoice, only $0.67 is profit; the rest is to cover the cost of goods.

Here is the eye-opener for most business owners and entrepreneurs, when you start to look at breakeven. Breakeven is simply what I have to sell in order to make enough profit to pay for the costs (expenses). So, if we go to a trade show and it costs us $750 (out of profit), we would have to sell $1,119.40 worth of products ($750/0.67) to make the $750 profit to pay for the show. When we hit $1,120.40, we would have finally made $1.00 of profit from the show.

Imagine if your costs were much higher, and your gross margin percentage was only 15 percent. This would mean for a trade show of $750, you would break even at $750/0.15, or $5,000! When you hit $5,001, you would have made your first dollar from the show! This sure makes you think differently when it comes to spending money in your business, because it works the same for hiring staff or any kind of expense. You pay your expenses from profit, not gross sales or revenue.

Continuing the example: If we were to hire a person at Make Your Mark, and we were to pay them $3,000 per month, our breakeven on this person would be $3,000/0.67, or $4,477.61 that we would have to make in gross sales or revenue in order to make enough profit to pay this person. There is a simple rule of thumb in business when it comes to sales staff: they have to sell three times their salary in order for you to have a winning staff member. If their salary is $70,000 per year, they would have to be bringing in at least $210,000. Then subtract $70,000 to pay them, another $70,000 for other office expenses, and the remaining $70,000 is profit for the company. This is the minimum a salesperson should generate. In fact, if they are doing more than five times their annual salary, keep them and pay them more. They are a huge asset to your business. The above is all very dependent on what your gross margins are as well and is fully explained at our Profit Warrior workshop, which gets you to really understand your numbers without the confusing accounting jargon.

Most business owners and entrepreneurs I encounter feel that they have broken even when they cover what it has cost them for the expense. Not true, as you can see from the calculations.

I trust that this has opened your eyes to what every dollar costs you in your business. Take the time to learn what the gross margins are in your business for each and every product and service, and for your business overall. This will tell you which products and services are the most profitable and where you should focus your attention.

I will leave you with a final thought: when I go out and buy coffee for my office, I may spend $20 for all our staff. But this comes out of profit, so I would have to generate $20/0.67, or $29.85 in sales to cover the costs of the coffee!

ASSEMBLE YOUR
MENTORSHIP TEAM

SUCCESS
SPOTLIGHT!
Ask is your task.

It is very important to find a few people who are willing to mentor you to achieve the success that you want. They may mentor you in very specific areas that you're looking for assistance in to take your business to the next level.

You may be asking, how do I find really good mentors? My answer to this is to find people whom you admire in the industry and who have success in the area that you are looking for success in, and ask them to mentor you. Some mentorship programs do cost money, and other programs may just be as simple as taking your mentor out to lunch once a month at your expense and asking them key questions that have come up for you during the month.

I have three mentors whom I personally work with and meet with on a regular basis. These three people have been instrumental in getting my businesses to the next level.

In order to be in contact with some of these top businesspeople, you will have to be very creative in your thinking. You may have to find out what their favorite restaurant or coffee shop is and hang out there regularly, with a possible chance of bumping into them and being able to maybe book an appointment or give them your card, and asking them if they would be interested in mentoring you. You may think this is uncomfortable and awkward, but I can tell you one thing: living outside of your comfort zone as an entrepreneur is your new life—get used to it!

Like I always say in sales, the most powerful four-letter word is NEXT. In business, the most important word is a three-letter word: ASK! Ask for what you want and develop that rhino hide so that you do not get taken down by "NOs." Remember, every "no" only gets you closer to a "yes."

One of our students recently wanted to get in touch with the owner of a major company. In fact, it was one of the major teams in the National Hockey League (NHL). She took the name of the team and decided to put the owner's last name before the "@" sign in an e-mail address, so that it read "last name@sportsteam.com." She received a response back from his assistant within twenty-four hours and later that week ended up having lunch with the owner of this NHL team. It all comes down to how creative you can be and how much you want to live outside of your comfort zone in order to get the results that you want. It's all about finding a solution and not giving in!

Having mentors in your life is very important. I will continue to have mentors to assist me in my business, and as my business shifts and changes, I will find additional mentors to help in those areas to grow me to the level of success where I would like to be. You have to do this continually for your own business as well.

BUILD RELATIONSHIPS WITH LIKE-MINDED
ENTREPRENEURS

SUCCESS
SPOTLIGHT!

Successful entrepreneurs associate with those who will push them to greater limits, higher levels of success, and more discomfort.

I would also highly recommend you find yourself a group of entrepreneurs and small-business owners who can support you and assist you as you grow your business. In all my years of being an entrepreneur, this is probably one of the most important considerations, as your success goes hand-in-hand with the people who you surround yourself with. When you surround yourself with very successful and like-minded entrepreneurs, the chances of achieving your goals, dreams, and financial security that you are looking for from your business will be directly influenced by the quality of entrepreneurs and small-business owners who you associate with.

When you first start out in your business, you may find it easier to hang around with business owners and entrepreneurs who are in the same place in their businesses as you. They may be start-up entrepreneurs or business owners with a few years' experience, but be careful not to hang out with people just because you find it easy and comfortable. Successful entrepreneurs associate with those who will push them to greater limits, higher levels of success, and more discomfort.

Take the time to build strong relationships with like-minded people. I cannot stress this enough because I know how much this can impact where you will be one year from now.

We have three types of groups that you should consider joining, as they are have taken thousands of business owners and entrepreneurs to the next level and keep them growing through powerful education: www.BESTMindset.com, www.KAPITSuccess.com, and www.MYMLegacy.com. Take a look and come out and see what we do. These groups have changed the lives and lifestyles of many business owners and entrepreneurs, and continue to do so.

KNOW THAT GREAT ATTITUDE
EQUALS GRATITUDE

SUCCESS
SPOTLIGHT!
The more you give gratitude, the more you will be given to be grateful for.

In my business I always talk about the two key reasons why we are so successful: getting up in the morning with a great attitude and, when you squeeze the words "great attitude" together, they combine to form the word "gratitude."

Having a great attitude in business is the difference between a success mindset and the mindset of somebody a year or two down the line who is still in their business but has not achieved outrageous results. A great attitude pushes you forward to more profit, success, learning, and time off in your business.

You read earlier about the difference in attitude between the two realtors. Both were highly qualified, and the only difference between sixty-seven CDs sold and none was attitude.

Great attitude and mindset go hand-in-hand with one another and really, at the end of the day, are pretty much one and the same thing. You have to be able to go out on a daily basis and be able to shift your attitude as quickly as possible. Of course you will have challenges and learning experiences along the way, but it's how quickly you shift your attitude that will directly impact how quickly you achieve results in your business. This goes hand-in-hand with being solution driven, which was mentioned earlier.

Gratitude, on the other hand, is something that is very important to me, and it is very simple to understand. My definition of gratitude is a thank you from deep within you. Louise Hay puts gratitude into perspective simply by saying that the more you give gratitude, the more items and situations will be given to you to be grateful for. Make sure that you're giving gratitude every single day for those who support you in your business, whether it is family, staff, colleagues, vendors, or your customers.

Remember your business does not exist without clients. Your clients are the ones who have given you the lifestyle that you are living, or will give it to you in the future. Be extremely grateful to them. I send out around twenty to thirty gratitude cards a month to absolutely anyone who has made an impact on my life—clients, friends, prospects, a waiter in a restaurant, a supplier who went above and beyond for a great meeting, companies that consider us for keynote addresses, etc. You will see that the more grateful you are for what you have, the more success will show up in your life and business.

CELEBRATE SUCCESSES

SUCCESS
SPOTLIGHT!
Celebrate the smallest
of successes.

It seems as if it's a part of our human nature to always focus on the negative aspect of our daily actions, rather than the positive. Most people don't realize that for every ten thoughts we have, nine are negative. It does take a ton of vigilant effort, focus, and self-awareness to be consistently positive and be putting out the right energy. We look at things in a way that often does not drive us forward, but holds us back. Celebrating successes no matter how small or big on a daily basis is crucial for massive entrepreneurial success.

What do you do on a daily basis to celebrate your successes?

Please take the time every single day to look at the successes that you have achieved and go out and celebrate those successes so that your body gets used to small incremental celebrations, because these eventually will lead into one large celebration of success. You do not necessarily have to spend money to celebrate your successes; it's the mere act of acknowledging your successes that is absolutely vital to more successes showing up in your business and in life.

In fact, we have our Big Dreams, Gratitude, Successes, and Happiness Journals that allow you to stay focused on all these items on a daily basis, because what you focus on most shows up in your life. Sadly, many people love to watch television before going to bed and are exposed to death, destruction, adultery, deceit, etc. When this is the last information that enters your brain before you retire for the night, whether consciously or subconsciously, guess what you focus on while you sleep? Yes, the negative! By journaling every day and realizing that no matter how much of a learning day you have had, there are definitely many successes to celebrate and things to be grateful for on a daily basis. When you want more success to show up in your life, focus on the successes you have had, and you will be surprised by what starts to happen, especially when you do it consistently for ninety days.

DEVELOP A
LEARNING PHILOSOPHY

SUCCESS
SPOTLIGHT!
Always show a
learning attitude!

There is an obvious reason why you are reading this book, and it's because you have a learning philosophy about life and business, and for that I congratulate you!

The most important skill in life is to always be learning. I believe that you continue to learn every day, and the more you learn, the less costly mistakes you will make and the quicker you will grow your business. Sadly, there are a lot of people who are struggling in their businesses or financially, and they seem to know it all. You talk with them and they have an answer for everything. In fact, sometimes they get upset with you when you challenge them concerning key items that they *say* they are doing, even when you know that if they were doing them, their business would definitely be in a different place.

The opposite of learning is stubborn pride. This is what I have seen to be the number-one killer of small businesses! Entrepreneurs do not ask for assistance, and they keep on doing the same thing and expecting a different result. We have clients who go through our Success System (www.MYMSuccess.com) and achieve extreme results. Even clients who are already extremely successful take our trainings and put their staff through our system so that they are all on the same page. Some go through, and when you see them a few months later, they have not implemented any of the strategies, techniques, or tools that you have taught them—and they wonder why they are not getting the results they want in their businesses. Some even have the audacity to blame the training, saying that they got nothing from it. If they knew everything that was in the training, then why are they still in the same place in their business?

Some even love the blame game and take the time to blame others for their lack of results. The only reason why you do not get results from a training or a course, whether it be with Make Your Mark or any company, is because you have not implemented what you have learned. There truly is only one person to blame, and that is the person who takes no action and expects to be hugely successful. You have to implement what you learn in order to achieve results—it's that simple!

I spend time going to other seminars, events, courses, retreats, and camps to learn more and improve my business for our students on an ongoing basis. I go with the attitude that I am in the audience to meet some great people and share with them what we do, and at the same time leave with some golden nuggets that I can use to enhance my own business and the systems for our students. I believe that I am in the event for a reason, and I will be learning what I am meant to learn and meet the people I am meant to meet. When you remain open to the possibilities in every way and form, you will be amazed at the results you will achieve.

In fact, many times I will be the last person to take a seat. I look around the room to see what seat is open, and I know that the universe has decided that this is the place I should sit! I meet the greatest people when I do this. At our Graduate Success Event, we have twenty display tables around the room for students to purchase to display their products at the event. One student arrived fifteen minutes before the table setup time and was adamant that she came early to get the best table, and we could not sway her as she was starting to get mad with us. At the end of the evening I spoke with her and said that all the tables are great and that if it were me, I would arrive in time to set up but let the universe decide which table I should have for the evening. The last table to set up that evening was a financial planner who ended up right next to another financial planner—they were both at peace with it because they knew that they were meant to be next to each other for a reason! Both financial planners achieved excellent results that evening. You have to realize that people buy from people they like and trust—not because you are the only financial planner in the room! This goes for all businesses. People buy from you because of the experience and how you make them feel, not because you have the best product or service!

We do not know it all, and if your business is challenged in certain areas, put your pride aside and get assistance from experts in those areas. I often get called into businesses when they are failing, and people expect me to wave a magic wand and change their business overnight. I have been able to do this in some cases, but in most I have to give the business owner the sad news that their situation is terminal. Yes, stubborn pride is like cancer to your business! If you do not ask for assistance and start learning when something is going wrong, you will find that by the time you ask for help, it's going to be too late. You will not have the finances to hire our Pro CEO Consulting services or attend any of our courses, and your business will die or be taken over by a shark for only a few cents on the dollar.

Please, always have a learning attitude no matter what! If it is a positive or negative situation, ask yourself, "What am I meant to learn?" Do this and you will always achieve success quicker.

My simple statement is, "The more you learn and implement, the quicker you grow, and the greater your success will be!"

DO NOT BE JUDGMENTAL

SUCCESS
SPOTLIGHT!
The highest energy
almost always wins!

Human beings are not born being judgmental, yet even during our first few years we can develop this tendency, which can dramatically impact us as adults later on in life. When we walk into a room full of people that we don't know, we will gravitate to a group that we judge to be similar to who we are ourselves.

When we go networking, we walk into a room and look around and decide in our heads who we are going to talk to and why. We look and our little voice inside our head comes up with some crazy statements:

1. Too old or too young to be my client.
2. I know somebody who looks like that and they are not successful.
3. Too bubbly for me.
4. That person seems arrogant (do not mistake this for confidence).
5. That person would be the easiest to talk to!

6. They are not dressed professionally.
7. I don't like the way they look.

All these key judgments stop us from talking with people who could easily become our next biggest client or even introduce us to people who would become our clients.

I went to a networking event a few years ago, and there was a lady on one side of the room in a wheelchair who was definitely in her seventies or even possibly early eighties, and nobody was talking with her. I had the judgment go through my head that said that we have no clients her age, she is probably retired, etc. These thoughts kept going through my mind until I said to myself, "Go and speak to her. What do you have to lose?" I went over to her, she was so enthralled that I would take the time to speak with her, and she introduced me to her three daughters who all have their own businesses—all three daughters are now clients of mine and have introduced us to their business associates and colleagues. It was a $30,000 contact that evening.

This may not happen every time you go out, but you will not know what results you can get until you take judgment out of the way and just go up to people and speak with them. It is actually one of the most powerful skills you can learn in life as a business owner.

The opposite of this is also true. Now that you understand that people judge you before you have even opened your mouth as to whether or not they will speak to you, the way you show up at public events is critical to your success. When you leave home or your office, you should be dressed for success. I promise you that you will get treated very differently at events when you show up in a suit rather than a pair of jeans—I don't care what industry you are in! The way you respect yourself is the judgment that people will have about you, whether consciously or subconsciously, and whether you talk with them or not.

We said before that the highest energy wins, and no matter how you are feeling, you need to show up with a smile and warm welcoming energy, even if you have just lost a massive order or had an argument with a spouse or business partner. Suck it up, put a smile on your face, and go out with a winning attitude.

Remember, the highest energy almost always wins!

SET OFFICE HOURS

SUCCESS
SPOTLIGHT!
Having office hours communicates to your clients that you are somebody who sticks to a plan and to commitments.

You must set office hours for your business, and even if you work from home, print them off and stick them up on the outside of your office door for your family to see. Just because you work from home does not mean that you can be continually interrupted. You may say, this is why you work from home, to have the flexibility. You have to remember when you are building your business, you have to put your sacrifice plan in place and ensure you are achieving your goals. I often hear about the family getting blamed for work that does not get done, poor follow-up, etc., when really it's the business owner who does not know how to say no to family and stick to their office hours.

During office hours, you only do business-building activities, just as if you would at an office job. If you know you are having family coming into town in a few months or that you want to go away, ensure you have a plan in place to be able to take the time off. Taking time off and living off lines of credit or credit cards for a few weeks is incredibly dangerous and can be financially devastating. Make your time off a reward for achieving certain targets in your business, and let your family know so they can assist by holding you accountable to achieving those targets and goals.

When you have office hours, it also lets your clients know that you have a structured business, like we spoke about earlier in the book. What it also tells your clients is when they can contact you and what the timeline would be to expect a response.

Unless you are in a profession where being on call is critical, then you should only take calls, e-mails, or text messages from clients and prospects during office hours.

If you are taking calls after hours, on weekends, or while on vacation and are irritated by it, you only have yourself to blame, as this is part of leadership. If you respond by answering the phone, e-mail, or text message, then you are condoning their contacting you during those times. And once they start, they believe they can do it continuously.

All my Pro CEO Consulting contracts have set hours for people to contact me, and I do stick to them. Remember, it's the rules again! Whose rules do you want to run according to: your own or the clients? If you are answering communications from clients outside of office hours, then you are letting them break your rules or make them for you!

Having office hours also communicates to your clients that you are somebody who sticks to a plan and to commitments. This is important, because if you break commitments to yourself or your family, they will undoubtedly think, "Will he do it to me?" Or they will abuse the situation and you may get irritated or upset, but again, you created the situation by not sticking to your hours.

Another reason why business owners take calls outside of set office hours is because you are chasing the money and or have been told that you may miss an incredible opportunity. Once you are strong at building relationships, people will wait for your return communication for a few hours or overnight. If you are anxiety driven and your smartphone controls your life, then you should ask yourself whether you are too focused on the money. How strong are your relationships, and who is truly in control of your life and business?

My family is everything to me, and I love them dearly and plan time off with them. When I am away, I take time away from technology—smartphone, tablet, laptop, etc.—and allow myself quality time with my family. This is the reason why I started my own business and can happily take off two to three months a year. I plan this time off at the beginning of the year and work my schedule, targets, and goals to ensure that during these times my cash flow is perfect and that my Pro CEO clients are all looked after, so that when I am away, they are not contacting me and vice versa. In fact, I have fun in my business and let my consulting clients know that if either of us contacts one another, then the person who made the contact whether via e-mail, phone, or text has to pay a $1,000 fine. This works wonderfully and does let people know that you are in full control of your business.

DO YOUR WEEKLY
SNAPSHOT

SUCCESS
SPOTLIGHT!
You must plan time each week to see where your business is.

Taking time away from your business is important. Look at it from the outside and see how on track you are to achieving your daily, weekly, monthly, and yearly goals. You must plan a time each week to look at where you are at and what needs to be done in order to get to where you want to be. I take a two-hour lunch every week by myself where I examine where I am in my business in relation to where I want to be, and I make a list of the items that need to be done to keep me on track. This is a vital part of running a successful business and one of the biggest reasons for having a plan or road map to where you want to be!

I book this time off and do not answer e-mails, phone calls, or any form of communications, as this is my focus on my own business and a commitment that I make to myself and my business.

MONITOR, MEASURE, AND ADJUST

SUCCESS
SPOTLIGHT!

Sometimes you are too close to your own business to see the solution.

Part of my Weekly Snapshot is monitoring, measuring, and adjusting what I am doing in my business, especially marketing activities. Marketing to me is fluid and something that is not cast in stone, as you can always make improvements and be testing different campaigns, headlines, brochures, flyers, website text, opt-in offers, etc. to determine the best marketing strategies for your business and the ones that are achieving the desired results.

If you are not monitoring and measuring your marketing, then you are flying by the seat of your pants and have no idea what is working and what is not! In fact, you are spending money without even knowing what your Return On Investment is.

You should be monitoring the ROI on the following:

- Business cards
- Brochures
- Website text
- Website analytics—what results are you getting from the traffic you receive?
- Opt-in on your website—how many user sessions are you getting for the number of opt-ins?
- E-mail broadcasts
- E-mail autoresponders
- E-mail drip campaigns
- Social media—what is your growth rate and response rate?
- Seminars and seminar sales
- Book sales and relatable downloads

- E-books, e-reports, etc. Free or purchased—what are the results?
- Trade shows
- Networking
- Public events

These should all be measured so that you know what results you are getting for the time and money that you are investing. You may decide that it's not costing you a lot of money and your time is your time and therefore you do not have to include it. Wrong—you have to include your time in all the activities you do. For example, if you go networking once a week and the total hours consumed are three hours from your home and back to your home, and your hourly rate is $50, then that event has cost you $150 plus the food, drinks, event cost, etc. If you are attending this event every week for a year, your total time investment alone is $7,500 a year. Then look at your gross margin percentage for your business using the same percentage as before: 66.67 percent. This would mean we break even at $7,500/0.67 = $11,194. This is the minimum you should be receiving over an annual basis in terms of leads, sales, etc. in order for it to be financially viable for your business to attend that networking event. You have to monitor your results to know if certain activities are worthwhile for your business.

Even if you get a massive response, you can always improve the results by testing something else. If the results do not deliver, then you go back to what was working—marketing is all about monitoring, measuring, and adjusting.

You may have a website, and it went live a few weeks, months, or years ago; what have you done to improve the results from your site? Are you frequently examining your website analytics to ensure you are getting traffic, and how are you converting the traffic into leads and sales? A dead site with no continual changes and enhancements is considered exactly that. You need to be progressive and ensure your site is linked to your blog and your social media.

You should also be monitoring, measuring, and adjusting your Cash Flow Predictor to ensure you are achieving your financial goals. It's very simple and can be compared to what sports teams do. All serious sports teams videotape their games to see what went right or wrong and what can be improved and worked on before the next game. This helps the team ensure they achieve the desired results of winning and having a loyal team of supporters continuing to follow and cheer for them.

Take the time each and every week to monitor, measure, and adjust, and you will start to see dramatic improvements in your results. You will also know where you need assistance to get you to the desired goals. If you have challenges understanding what needs to be adjusted, ask for advice from mentors, trainers, associates, and consultants so that they can assist you. Remember, you must only take advice from those who have a track record and been successful in the area that you are seeking advice in. Most of all, ask for advice and do not let stubborn pride hold you back. To me, there is no dumb question in business! We have all had to learn along the way, and being open to learning is a huge asset to growing your business.

I personally hire business experts to assist me in areas of my business where I am finding challenges. It is often more difficult to see the solutions when you are so close to your own business. Sometimes, what I can see as a quick solution for a Pro CEO client, I cannot see for myself. I have spent tens of thousands of dollars on business courses, coaches, and consultants, and I have surrounded myself with great entrepreneurs and business owners, because I know I can get the answers I need from them without wasting a ton of valuable time or money.

EXPOSE YOUR BUSINESS

SUCCESS
SPOTLIGHT!
Where you hang out will dictate your results!

One of the first courses we have in our Success System at Make Your Mark is called Exposure Warrior, which teaches you that you must be exposing your business online and offline. Online networking includes all the aspects of social media, and offline includes going to public events like trade shows, networking events, boards of trade, chambers of commerce, cocktail parties, seminars, courses, vacations, etc. Yes, anywhere you come into contact with other people I consider to be a networking and business-building opportunity.

Whenever you are in contact with people, you should be professional, have a great attitude, and carry business cards with you. A certain part of this book was written in Los Cabos, Mexico, while I was on vacation with my family. I took business cards with me because I knew people would be talking to me about business, as I love to socialize by the pool and in restaurants. It's fun to introduce people to what we do, because if they are business owners, then I know we can assist them. In fact, I choose to vacation at more higher-end resorts because it will dictate the quality of people that I may encounter, and it always does! This goes hand-in-hand with whom and where you hang out.

I have a good friend who owns a hotel and does many construction projects around Vancouver, and he goes to a seven-star hotel in Dubai every now and again for a couple of nights to meet people who may have the money to fund some of these multimillion-dollar projects that he is busy with. The cost per night for an average room at this hotel is $5,000 and goes up to $100,000 for the presidential suite; he only pays industry rates, which is $2,500 per night. He knows with airfares and everything included that it's going to cost him around $10,000 for the weekend away.

You may consider this exorbitant, but it really is a two-day networking event, because at this hotel you will only find extremely wealthy people. He spends time in their bar and restaurant networking and talking to people, and over the course of two days he finds all the money he needs. This is a great example of figuring out where the people you want to hang out with will be and going out and finding them.

What could you do for your business? Remember, nothing is impossible! The only impossibilities come from your mindset, which can hinder you or place hurdles in your way.

EXAMINE YOUR
ENVIRONMENT

SUCCESS
SPOTLIGHT!
Life is a book and, people come into it for a reason.

You have to be careful with this topic, as there is a fine line between being selective and being judgmental—i.e., being too selective with whom you surround yourself with and where you hang out.

Find people who are more successful or even substantially more successful than you are, and you will watch your results skyrocket. The best way to describe this is through another sport example, and this time I will use tennis. When you play tennis with somebody who is significantly more advanced than you are, it raises your game and pushes your comfort zone. The corollary of this is that when you are a strong player and you continuously play against weaker opponents, it will reduce the quality of your game—yes, you will not stay at the same level.

I am very selective of the people whom I allow into my circle of friends, as I know how much of an impact this can have on my life and my business. When I am doing business and I share an idea or challenge I am having with a businessperson who is more successful than I am, they push me to raise my game and get out of my comfort zone. With a weaker business owner, they may say that things are okay and that you should not feel too bad—completely allowing you to accept the lot that you are in!

Be very careful who you have speaking into your life and business. After reading this, you may be thinking that you may have to say goodbye to a few friends and find some new ones. Some of these may be long-term friendships, and you must decide whether or not these friends are adding to your tennis game of life or pulling you down. Ask yourself the question, "Do these friends support me, and with them in my life will I be further ahead in twelve months' time, or the same, or even worse off?" If you did not say "further ahead," then I would ask you to really consider why you have them in your life.

I will give you another analogy from my incredibly gifted mother-in-law, Barbara Lovell, who told me that life is a book. Yes, we all have our own life book, and within the book we have people who come into our lives for a sentence, a paragraph, a chapter, a few chapters, or the entire book. We just have to realize and accept that they do not have to be there for the entire book, and also understand that even if they came in for a short period of time, it was for a reason. That reason may have been for them to introduce us to someone else, to teach us a lesson, to give us a learning experience, etc. Once you understand this you will realize that you should not guilt yourself about maintaining friendships or relationships that are not feeding your growth, energy and success.

You may say that family is a tough one, and it is because they are your blood and you must maintain relationships with them. I absolutely agree, but if they are not driving you forward. Then create your sacrifice plan and let them know that you are not being rude or avoiding them, but that all you are doing is building your business.

PAY IT FORWARD

SUCCESS
SPOTLIGHT!
Do not give with expectation!

I find working with charities and not-for-profits to be extremely uplifting, as you are doing something for the community and making a difference in other people's lives for no financial gain. You also get to meet other amazing business owners and entrepreneurs who love giving because they fully understand the universal laws, and one of them is give and you shall receive. You have to remember this when you give from your heart, and not just doing it while expecting something in return. When you expect something in return, you will find that very little ever materializes. I do a ton of work with the Surrey Food Bank Society (www.SurreyFoodBank.org) in Canada, as it assists thousands of people on a monthly basis and it gets me out of my daily routines to go and have some fun while making a difference. Even if you cannot afford to give financially in your business, take the time to give your time to a local organization—there are thousands of people in need.

I used to have a real ego attitude towards charities that give handouts, because I always believed that the more you give, the bigger the hand gets, until I met David Mann, who has become a good friend of mine. He said to me, "Colin, when you judge what the people do with the gift you are giving them, two things happen: you rob yourself of the kindness with which it was done, and you are giving with expectation!" This completely changed my thought process, because Dave also said to me that whatever they do with the gift you give them, that is 100 percent their choice because where they are right now in their life is the perfect place for them, and who are we to judge?

CHAPTER 7

TROUBLESHOOTING: NINE KEY AREAS WHERE ENTREPRENEURS' SUCCESS **OFTEN STALLS**

As you become more successful in your business, you will start to forget what it took you to get there, and you may even sabotage further success. In many instances, some of the concepts below are very simple, yet I have seen them stall entrepreneurs' success on many occasions. My goal is to make you aware of them to ensure you continue on your path of massive entrepreneurial success. Most recipes do not have a section for troubleshooting, but many of us who thought we were following the instructions perfectly, and still ended up with a mess, sure wish they did!

ARE YOU STILL SELLING?

SUCCESS
SPOTLIGHT!
Your customers buy from
you because they like you!

During my Pro CEO Consultations, one of the first questions I ask a business owner who has been doing well and now seems to be ailing is, "When did you take yourself out of the sales role, or what have you changed in your sales process?" In many instances they have gone out and hired a salesperson who is not as passionate about the business and have pulled themselves out of the sales role either completely or to a large extent.

You have to remember you have built all the relationships and cultivated them over months and years prior to staff joining you. Your customers bought from you because they liked you. This is a tough transition in any small business, and I know there comes a time when you need to make a decision: do I step out of sales, or do I hire a general manager to report to me and run the operations of my business? This is a very important question. I would never take yourself out of the sales role totally, otherwise you start to hear comments like, "Are we not good enough for

Colin to visit us anymore?" These comments can seriously hurt your business.

Handing over the sales reigns does take a very specific strategy and must be done with great customer care and outstanding communication.

PARALYSIS BY ANALYSIS

SUCCESS
SPOTLIGHT!
You must manage all
aspects of your business!

A growing business is exciting and can take a ton of your time to implement processes, procedures, and policies in order to ensure that you have a very well-defined structure for your business. At the same time, you do not want to neglect sales, as this is the heart of your business and what has gotten you the success you have achieved so far.

Plus, most entrepreneurs are not great at spending hours on administrative functions like bookkeeping, cash flow, data entry, database management, costing, etc. In fact, most of them have no interest.

When you get to a stage of hiring, write down all the tasks you love to do and those you dislike. Then write a job description around the tasks you dislike and find the required resources to do it for you. Please remember that you have to manage all aspects of your business. This does not mean that because you have delegated that you do not have to understand or manage all areas of the business.

CASH IS OXYGEN:
ARE YOU BREATHING?

SUCCESS
SPOTLIGHT!
All decisions impact cash flow.

This area of business totally fascinates me because you are in business to make money, yet the management of money is done very poorly. Once you have completed the Cash Flow Predictor™ from the previous section, you should not make a single decision in your business if the scenario is not run through your Cash Flow Predictor to determine the financial impact that your decision has on your business. In some businesses you may be monitoring your cash flow on a daily basis, some weekly, but at minimum you should be doing it monthly.

The saddest statement I hear from entrepreneurs is that their accountant or bookkeeper is going to tell them if they made money this month or year! This is no way to run a business, unless you have a full-time chief financial officer. Learn how to understand your numbers so that you understand profitability, margins, and costs, to be fully in control of your business and the results you are achieving!

HOOKED ON BRANDING

SUCCESS
SPOTLIGHT!
Your number-one marketing
and sales asset is you!

Let me tell you something: Branding is for the big boys like Gillette, Coca Cola, Pepsi, and Nike. You have to have very deep pockets to effectively brand your business, and I mean deep, billion-dollar pockets. Sadly, when you first start out, you will meet graphic designers, advertising agencies, and marketers that will tell you that you have to create a branding strategy and select the most appropriate logo, colors, etc. for your business.

I do not completely disagree with them; all I can say is that in the beginning, your number-one marketing and sales asset is YOU! You can have the fanciest logo, website, or brochure, but if people do not like you, they will not buy from you. It's that simple! When I first started Make Your Mark, I had no brochure or website for the first twelve months. I decided that I would conserve my cash for solid money-making marketing initiatives. Once I had built a strong clientele and a good healthy cash flow, I then added a powerful website, social media strategy, marketing banners, tools, and more.

When you first start out, you need a great attitude, professional dress code, business cards, and a ton of confidence, and you will be set.

IT'S NOT THE ECONOMY—
IT'S YOU!

SUCCESS
SPOTLIGHT!
The economy is always changing; are you?

This is a vital area and probably the most common one where business owners fall over. When you first start out, you do not have a ton of clients, and you can do all your cold calling, networking, and follow-up calls on a daily basis, but as you get busy you start to put this aside or on the backburner. You make the excuses or justification that you are too busy to network or cold call or follow up. Typically, three months later, your business slows because you have finished all the work you were doing for your clients and instead of taking responsibility and realizing that you have not been keeping your sales pipeline full, you say, "The economy has changed, or people are not buying." This is often as a result of your actions!

Nothing has happened, other than you stopped filling your sales pipeline. When you take time out each week to look at your business and monitor, measure, and adjust, look at what you are doing to keep your sales pipeline full! At Sales Warrior we train you on how to do this effectively and on an ongoing basis. Otherwise, you will experience the peaks and troughs in your business. Keeping your sales pipeline full and working on it on a daily basis, no matter how busy you are, will smooth out the cash flow in your business and make your business a lot more manageable.

ADAPT OR DIE

SUCCESS
SPOTLIGHT!
When the economy changes, you should be ahead of the curve and not surprised.

Speaking of the economy, the economy is always changing and will fluctuate depending on what is happening with unemployment rates, debt loadings, interest rates, commodity prices, housing prices, and overall consumer confidence.

These fluctuations happen on a daily basis and are highly influenced by rumors and what is happening in the media and world politics. My question to you is, are you shifting with the economy? Are you doing your research and being prepared for what is coming and listening to reports by economists and demographers so that you can prepare accordingly? When the economy changes, you should be ahead of the curve and not be surprised. Sadly, most entrepreneurs are taken by surprise and lose a fortune, and in some cases even go bankrupt.

I have a very good friend who is a business coach, and she was assisting a gentleman with his real estate investing business a few years back. She had never built a real estate business herself and was only holding him accountable to achieving his dreams of owning a large real estate portfolio and keeping him on track according to his own business plan.

This gent got into a situation where he had achieved most of his real estate goals; the only thing was that he was highly leveraged and had substantial loans from a variety of banks to cover his assets. Sadly, the market cratered in 2008 and he lost everything. He was not looking at the future and adding in some wiggle room to ensure that he would not be taken out if real estate prices plummeted or if interest rates skyrocketed—he went bankrupt and is now rebuilding his life.

I want you to be continuously monitoring what is going on in the marketplace, looking at what the future holds for your products and/or services and how you would be impacted if the economy suddenly took a downturn.

This may be the difference in shifting your focus from one geographical area to another (you may have to look at what other states, provinces, or cities may be more appropriate to target where the economies are healthier), or adding a product that is more in demand during down economies. This is not distraction by bright, shiny objects but more preparing for success no matter what the economy is doing.

Be aware that the economy is going to change—are you ready for it, and most of all, is your business prepared for it?

FIXING WHAT ISN'T
BROKEN

SUCCESS
SPOTLIGHT!

Be very careful about what products and services you are going to add, as they may dilute your focus from your money machine.

As your business grows and prospers, you are going to start to hire people and have them take over certain roles in your company. Your business is going to become highly structured and process driven. You will go to work and things will become very systematic—and for most entrepreneurs, this will drive you crazy. We all thrive as entrepreneurs because of our love for creating and watching things build from the ground up. What drives most of us crazy is when things are built, and now we have a company that is doing well. Soon we decide that we need to change it, and we get creative because we are bored. But do not fix something that is not broken.

A great analogy is that most entrepreneurs like to find the land, find the best way to prepare the soil, source the best quality seeds, plant them, and watch the harvest grow and reap the rewards. Once this becomes a proven process of doing the same thing year in and year out, most entrepreneurs go out to see how they can add additional products or services and often dilute their interest in their core profitable business. I am not saying that you should not be creative, but when you have a proven process that is making you significant money, you should be very selective about what products or services you are going to add that will take away time from your money machine.

LEARNING TO
RELINQUISH CONTROL

SUCCESS SPOTLIGHT!

When you allow key people to make decisions in your business, your business becomes more valuable.

Bringing on the right people and allowing them to assist you in building your business is vital to growing and creating the legacy that you want to leave behind. The toughest parts for most entrepreneurs are:

- Finding people who they believe will be good enough to do the job. In other words, finding people who have the same passion as them.
- Trusting people enough to do certain tasks within their business. And once they find people to do the tasks, being able to let them do the tasks in their own style without having to micromanage them.

This for me was one of the biggest challenges and letting go of certain items has taken time, but it has allowed me to focus on where my business is going and being the true visionary that I have always been.

In some cases, you have to realize what your talents and strengths are and hire people around you to complement you. If you love sales and going out and chasing the deal, then you may hire an office manager or general manager to run the operations of your business while you go out and do what you are excellent at. You do not necessarily have to be the president of your business—the biggest asset you have is to decide what you need in order to grow your business. You can still have the president reporting to you, but the president can run and operate the company on a daily basis to maximize the potential of what you have created, and you continue to be creative and have fun.

I often say to business owners and entrepreneurs that one of the biggest challenges you will face is trusting people to do certain functions in your business. But once you master this, it is so rewarding. You start to realize that others do have talents outside of you, and now you are starting to build value in your business because the business is no longer solely reliant on you to run. This makes your business a valuable asset and saleable to a third party. You truly become a business owner as compared to being self-employed. If you do not allow this to happen, you will almost certainly not hit your goals and dreams!

BECOMING "VITAMIN C" DEFICIENT— IN COMMITMENT,
CASH, AND CLIENTS

SUCCESS
SPOTLIGHT!
Put away enough cash to carry you through the lean times, because they do come.

As your business continues to grow and prosper, you have to ensure that you maintain your commitment to the business. Businesses do not just keep growing by themselves unless you have the right people in place, and you still have to manage them in order to keep your finger on the pulse and keep everyone growing the business the way it was intended. Often entrepreneurs start up new ventures, which is excellent, but if you have not completely unplugged yourself from the existing business, all you start to do is dilute your focus by chasing something new and exciting, which can often cause a very profitable business to start ailing.

In the same vein, as you start to grow your business and cash flow improves dramatically, you need to be extremely careful to watch your spending habits. It's very easy to start spending money on items that you really don't need (luxury items). I often ask myself the following question, "If I were in start-up mode, would I be considering this purchase or spending the money I am about to spend?" If my answer to this question is no, then I really have to look at my Cash Flow Predictor and determine that the investment or purchase I am about to make is not going to dramatically impact the financial position of the business. I know you will get to the position where cash is extremely flush in your business, and all I ask is that you be smart enough to put away enough cash to carry you through some lean times, because they do come.

CHANGING HABITS
TAKES TIME

SUCCESS
SPOTLIGHT!
Faith is trust without thought.

I spoke earlier about habits and addictions and how they truly impact your life and business, especially the non-supportive ones. Many trainings out there say that it only takes thirty days to create a new habit. I disagree with that somewhat, in that I believe it takes thirty days to get you on a path to creating a new habit.

Habits are key behaviors that have taken you years, if not decades, to build and reinforce, and we expect in thirty days to completely shift them to new habits? I agree with creating new supportive habits and doing them on a daily basis to ensure you reprogram your body, mind, and cells to realize that change is taking place.

The challenge is that the human mind is designed to keep us safe and easily goes back to the old habits that it has become accustomed to—when you are tired, mentally drained, or in a state of high emotion, I often find that old habits creep back in really quickly and with ease.

When I first arrived in Canada, I knew that we had to drive on the opposite side of the road, because in South Africa we drive on the left-hand side. I quickly acclimatized and started driving on the right-hand side. After being here for nearly eleven years, I was leaving a function (completely sober) with my wife and heading home from an event when she said to me, "You cannot be serious! You are on the wrong side of the road!" I was stunned, as she was 100 percent right. I was completely unaware that I was on the wrong side of the road. Thank goodness there were no cars coming in the opposite direction.

This really got me thinking!

I have been habitually driving on the right side of the road now for almost fifteen years, yet I easily went back to my old habit when I was extremely tired. I had driven on the left-hand side of the road in South Africa for over ten years, but I had also been driven around by my parents and had gotten used to the left-hand side of the road for over two decades. So, I had nearly three times more exposure to the left-hand side of the road than the right-hand side.

I know that the mind is extremely powerful and that you can do almost anything with a shift in mindset. Yet, in states of high emotion or exhaustion, your body seems to simply revert back to old habits. It takes significant work to convert poor habits into supportive habits, and when you are feeling down, it takes even more focus and attention to stay on track to ensure you do not revert back to your old habits. You really have to reprogram your personal mindset computer to focus on success.

You have to practice new habits each and every day and really get them ingrained at a cellular level for them to be truly effective. It does take focus, persistence, and determination, and once mastered you will achieve life-altering habits that will support you in achieving increased success.

CONCLUSION

THE ENTREPRENEUR SUCCESS RECIPE

People will forget what you said, people will forget what you did, but people will never forget how you made them feel.
—Maya Angelou

Now that we've fully covered the preparation, the key ingredients, the instructions, and the troubleshooting tips of the Entrepreneurial Success Recipe, here's a shorthand version for you to refer to easily as you put it into practice! Read it through, understand it, refer back to this book when necessary, and keep this recipe visible at all times to remind you of what you need to focus on, or what skill sets or habits you need to work on, in order to achieve the success that you so deserve in your life and business!

To bake the perfect entrepreneur:

- Take one person.
- Add a massive HUNGER for success.
- Add a vivid vision and laser focus.
- Turn up the heat to maximum discomfort.
- Void the environment of toxic influences.
- Find a setting with consistent and unwavering support.
- Be extremely tenacious until goal is achieved.
- Progress until perfect growth and profit is obtained.
- Avoid costly distractions.
- Understand all costs.
- Add powerful resources.
- Relinquish control.
- Maximize income and time off!

Once you have achieved the above, you will be a very successful entrepreneur! You can also double and triple the recipe by going out and building other businesses while your existing venture grows and prospers.

After a month of applying the Entrepreneurial Success Recipe to your business, go back and take the Entrepreneurial Test again to see how well you've done at developing new skills and habits and what you still need to work on in order to achieve massive success. I would highly recommend taking the test every month for the first six months and thereafter every quarter to ensure you are staying on track in following the Entrepreneur Success Recipe. You can also use this book as a reference for all stages in your business.

To your success in achieving your Entrepreneurial MBA—Mega Bank Account!

ADDITIONAL RESOURCES FOR YOUR SUCCESS

Learn More about Applying the Entrepreneurial Success Recipe to Your Business: Attend the Business Mastery—Power in YOU! Event

If you would like to take your business to the next level and learn how to apply the Entrepreneurial Success Recipe in a more personalized way, our three-day Business Mastery—Power in YOU! event was designed just for you. These are the key ingredients you will learn at the event:

- Powerful words that destroy you and your success.
- How to think like the wealthy and drive your personal and professional results to extreme levels of success. Eighty percent of success comes from the inner game of psychology, and 20 percent comes from your skill and knowledge.
- Why knowledge and skill are not the keys to success.
- Why your own mind is often your worst enemy.
- How to train yourself for natural and automatic success.
- How to break through all your invisible sales and income barriers.

- The cause of virtually all financial problems and all financial success.

If you've bought this book or received it as a gift, you can attend this event for FREE! If you've received this book as a gift from a Make Your Mark student, you'll see a Success Number entered in the box below. Please use this Success Number when confirming your complimentary attendance for the Business Mastery—Power in YOU! three-day event. Full details for the Business Mastery event can be found under LIVE EVENTS on the www.MYMSuccess.com website or by calling our office at (+1) 778-565-4090.

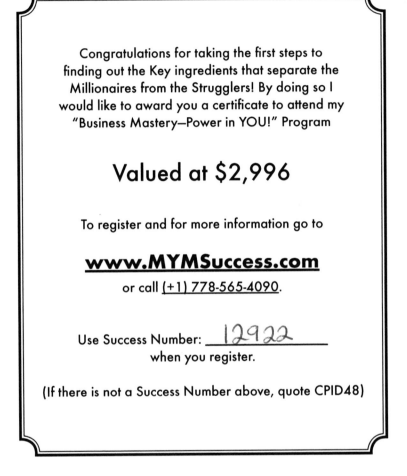

Congratulations for taking the first steps to finding out the Key ingredients that separate the Millionaires from the Strugglers! By doing so I would like to award you a certificate to attend my "Business Mastery—Power in YOU!" Program

Valued at $2,996

To register and for more information go to

www.MYMSuccess.com
or call (+1) 778-565-4090.

Use Success Number: __12922__
when you register.

(If there is not a Success Number above, quote CPID48)

OTHER RESOURCES FROM
COLIN SPRAKE AND
MAKE YOUR MARK

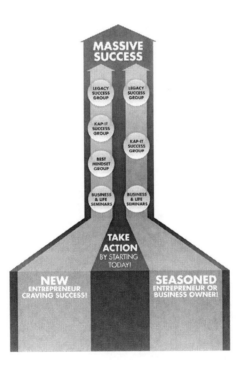

Make Your Mark offers a specialized process and system of experiential courses and groups in all areas of personal growth and business to maximize the results in your life and business. All events are designed to help students learn, apply, and develop the key ingredients in the Entrepreneur Success Recipe to become hugely successful entrepreneurs, which means making significant money and have maximum time off.

Here is a list of the courses and groups that are part of the dynamic SUCCESS SYSTEMS we designed to help you achieve maximum results and abundance. Visit www.MYMSuccess.com to sign up or learn more.

BUSINESS SUCCESS SYSTEM: Seminars

BUSINESS ESSENTIALS

Business Mastery—Power in YOU! (three days)

This seminar will transform your financial future forever. You will learn how to win the money game both in life and business, and achieve outrageous levels of success to live the lifestyle you want!

Business Plan 101 (one day)

A business with a set of crystal-clear core values and a written plan achieves massive results. This course takes you through a detailed plan of generating a one-page business plan for your business! Vital for all business owners and entrepreneurs.

Exposure Warrior (one day)

Get your business out into the marketplace quickly and effectively with unbelievable results. You'll learn key growth strategies that will have your business growing more quickly than you ever believed possible.

Sales Warrior (two days)

Two days of learning the opening and closing techniques to make more sales than you ever have. Double your sales in sixty to ninety days with true heart connection!

Marketing Warrior (two days)

Create marketing materials that WOW your prospect and turn them into paying customers! Learn an entire step-by-step process that you can use for the rest of your life and in any business!

BUSINESS BRILLIANCE

Profit Warrior (one day)

Learn how to manage your money like a multimillion-dollar business. Understand how and when to find money long before you need it! By the end, you will be in complete control of your business.

Winning Websites 1: Maximizing Traffic (one day)

A website without traffic is like having a salesperson who does not sell! You will understand how to get onto the first page of Google and dramatically improve the traffic to your site.

Business Excellence (three days)

This annual event has six guest business experts who will walk you through key areas of your business to maximize profit, minimize taxes, and protect you and your business.

Hire/Fire 101 (one day)

The biggest liability after your mindset are the people you hire to assist you in your business. There are critical items you need to have in place to ensure you hire the right people and keep them. This course takes you through everything you need to know around hiring, firing, and working with subcontractors to the maximum benefit of your business.

BUSINESS ELITE

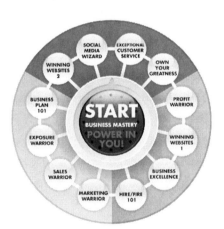

Exceptional Customer Service (one day)

Turn your customers into raving fans by giving them a memorable experience every time they buy from you. This is the quickest way to growing your client base and income.

Winning Websites 2: Converting Traffic (one day)

Once you have turned on the traffic faucet, you need to be able to convert it into leads and money for your business. You will learn the key connection strategies to maximizing conversion of prospects into clients online.

Social Media Wizard (one-and-a-half day)

This course teaches you how to utilize your time more effectively by turning your social media activities into lead generation and income. There are three secrets to a solid social media system that will be shared to turn your activities into income.

Own Your Greatness (three days)

These three days will take your experience at Business Mastery—Power in YOU! to an entirely new level of manifesting the results you want on a daily basis and achieving significant levels of financial success and time off!

GROUPS

BEST Mindset Groups

Business education is an essential part of a growing business, especially during the start-up phase. These groups meet every two weeks to set goals, hold you accountable, and assist with business education, tools, understanding and discussing challenges, and keeping your sales pipeline full. These are absolutely essential for entrepreneurs and business owners without staff and/or in start-up phase.

KAP-IT Success Groups

Meeting monthly as your own personal board of advisors, these groups are comprised of six established business owners who want to go to the next level of success. It's all about business owners assisting business owners with life and business experiences to ensure you save tens of thousands of dollars and maintain balance between work and life. There is an application process to belong to a KAP-IT Success Group, because you have to be focused on results and have set items in place and be willing to be held extremely accountable.

Legacy Groups

Colin lives by the statement, "Build a dynasty, leave a legacy." Only two of these groups will ever exist and have ten highly successful businesses in them. Quarterly retreats are held for four days with business experts, life coaches, and personal mentors of Colin to assist business owners to put in place all the structures and systems for succession planning and truly leaving a legacy. Membership is by application only.

LIFE SUCCESS SYSTEM: SEMINARS

Life Mastery 1: Million-Dollar Relationships (three days)
Life Mastery 2: Live, Love, and Laugh (three days)
Success Mastery 1: Pursuit of Passion (three days)

GROUPS

Abundance Tracker and Coaching
Circle of LIFE

ABOUT THE AUTHOR

Colin Sprake is a Extreme Business Builder who fully understands how to build businesses in any kind of economy. He has decades of experience in both male- and female-dominated markets and has worked in over seventy countries.

Born in South Africa and having both an engineering and business degree, he brought his expertise to North America in 1998 and is now a Canadian citizen and resides in South Surrey, BC.

Colin is a vibrant speaker with a huge heart who has helped thousands of small businesses and entrepreneurs. He captivates his audience by delivering marketing, sales, and business strategies, and personal growth tools in very simple and easy-to-understand formats.

One thing Colin always guarantees his audiences is that you will walk away from his presentations, no matter how long or short, with tools you can use immediately in your life and business.

You can contact Colin directly via email at ColinESR@ MYMSuccess.com. He loves to hear success stories from what you have implemented from the book and his events!

LOOKING FOR A RESULTS-DRIVEN, ACTION-ORIENTED,
INSPIRATIONAL SPEAKER?

Colin Sprake, the Business Acceleration Renegade, is an internationally recognized keynote speaker & trainer, and is known in the media as an expert on small business trends, hyper-growth strategies for small business and leveraging personal power to accelerate your life.

Colin works with organizations and individuals to develop personalized long-term strategies for success. He approaches his speaking engagements the same way, everything is customized based upon the type of audience and goals you want to achieve for your group.

Colin entertains, stimulates thought and acts as a catalyst for many who are stuck getting in their own way of tremendous success. His programs are high energy, filled with activities and educational with content based upon his own personal experience of building several multi-million dollar businesses.

Topics Include:

1. Life Success Recipe
2. Entrepreneur Success Recipe
3. Heart Sell Not Hard Sell!
4. Winning in Any Economy.
5. Business With Soul!

Call (+1) 778-565-4090
to book Colin for your next event!

CPSIA information can be obtained at www.ICGtesting.com
Printed in the USA
BVOW07s2009211214

380104BV00001B/1/P